NEVER GIVE UP

How to Cultivate the Right Mindset & Habits to Achieve Success & Overcome Obstacles

KEV WEBSTER

Published 2024

Front Cover Photo Kev Webster 2005

The author and publisher specifically disclaim all responsibility for any liability, loss or risk, personal or otherwise, that is incurred as a consequence, directly or indirectly, of the use and application of any of the contents of this book.

Copyright © 2024 by Kev Webster

All rights reserved.

No portion of this book may be reproduced in any form without written permission from the publisher or author except as permitted by U.S. copyright law.

Table of Contents

CHAPTER 1
WHY I WROTE THIS BOOK..................1

CHAPTER 2
THE POWER OF ENTHUSIASM..................9

CHAPTER 3
THE POWER OF RITUALS..................17

CHAPTER 4
WHAT ROLE DO YOU PLAY IN YOUR LIFE THEATRE?..................23

CHAPTER 5
TAKE A COURSE AND LEARN SOMETHING NEW..................29

CHAPTER 6
THAT NEW SKILL COULD CHANGE YOUR LIFE – IT DID MINE..................33

CHAPTER 7
WHY PERFECTIONISM IS THE END OF PROGRESS..................41

CHAPTER 8
HOW YOUR SOFT ENVIRONMENT DEFINES YOU 49

CHAPTER 9
YOUR HARD ENVIRONMENT REFINES YOU 55

CHAPTER 10
YOUR SKILLS AND TOOLS ENVIRONMENT
ENABLES YOU 61

CHAPTER 11
GETTING YOUR MINDSET ALIGNED 65

CHAPTER 12
GOOD DISTRACTIONS GET THINGS DONE 73

CHAPTER 13
THE POWER OF WORD ASSOCIATION 79

CHAPTER 14
YOU BECOME WHAT YOU THINK ABOUT 83

CHAPTER 15
YOU NEED TO AVOID CRITICAL EXPOSURE
OVERLOAD 89

CHAPTER 16
OUR BIG PROBLEM WITH JUDGMENTS 95

CHAPTER 17
MAKING YOUR MASTER PLAN 101

CHAPTER 18
MYTH BUSTING YOUR SUPERSTITIONS 107

CHAPTER 19
LEARNING TO CELEBRATE YOUR ACHIEVEMENTS 113

CHAPTER 20
TALKING AS THERAPY 119

CHAPTER 21
HOW TO ADOPT THE HABITS OF SUCCESS 127

CHAPTER 22
BEYOND YOUR MASTER PLAN 131

CHAPTER 23
BE GRATEFUL EVERY DAY 135

CHAPTER 24
OBSERVE THE THINGS YOU DO, SAY, AND THINK ... 139

CHAPTER 25
TUNE OUT THOSE DESTRUCTIVE DISTRACTIONS ... 143

CHAPTER 26
PARTING SHOTS 149

Chapter 1
Why I Wrote This Book

Ask yourself this question: 'Why do I give up on my dreams?' Discovering the answer will enable you to change the behaviors and thought processes that hold you back. That is why I wrote this book – to help you focus on your path ahead. When you look forward and master your thoughts and actions – the world responds in ways that are presently unimaginable.

Why? Because your dreams and ambitions nurture and feed the seeds of your future.

I want to clarify from the start that this is a self-help book, not a 'shelf help' book. To make change happen, you must act and apply the principles and ideas I share. No amount of good intention, visualization, or dreaming will outweigh the results of taking positive action. Moreover, positive action is closely aligned with your **master plan.**

Do not worry, I have dedicated a whole chapter to help you create your own personal masterplan later in this book.

Why did I decide to call this book 'Never Give Up'? The short answer is something that my son said to me after I lost my business and family home. As we enjoyed our regular lunch get-together, I shared that I'd recently learned how to build websites and earn money online. He smiled at me and said, *"If there's one thing I've learned from you, Dad, it is to never give up"*. At the time, I didn't think much about it apart from that it was a wonderful thing for him to say - on reflection, it is one of the most fundamental survival tools everyone should learn and teach their children. At the time, I was 42, had lost my business, was going through bankruptcy, and my wife had left me - things looked grim.

Instead of wallowing in my own self-pity and feelings of failure, I took a long, hard look at myself and came to this startling conclusion. ***If my thoughts and actions have brought me to this desperate place, I need to change my thoughts and actions to get different results in the future.***

There is something else you need to know about me. This wasn't my first business failure. Since the age of 21, I have lost two other businesses. You could say I was very successful at failing in business.

The original title for this book was PERSEVERANCE; when I came up with that title, I thought I'd made a breakthrough and felt smugly pleased with myself. As you will discover throughout this book, my approach to creativity, including writing this book, is fluid and mostly unstructured. Front cover ideas come and go, chapter titles evolve, and even the book's subtitle changed slightly after I had written the 30 thousandth word. In a later chapter, you will discover why it is crucial for you to get comfortable with flexibility and how fluidity of thought will help you overcome the mental rigidity that often manifests itself as perfectionism and procrastination.

"If perfectionism comes at a price, time is the currency we spend pursuing it" Kev Webster, 2016

Throughout this book, you will quickly realize that I do not and will not spend time focusing on negatives. The truth is, we can all recognize unhelpful repeated behaviors if we are honest with ourselves. The journey you are about to take will encourage and guide you to make new habits and attitudes to help you transform your life. Slowly but surely, you will start to feel and see different results. *If you enjoy dwelling on the past, this book is not for you. If you are more committed to being a victim or enjoy moaning about how shit your life is. Save your money.*

This book is about taking responsibility for your future *(being capable and responsive) and* working with all the tools available. Some of these tools will be familiar to you but may have been used destructively in the past. That's about to change. If you are willing to unlearn old habits and learn some new ones – your life will be transformed.

Within the first three chapters of this book, you will discover the immense and transformative power of enthusiasm, you will see why it's important to adopt some interesting and new daily rituals and you will explore the roles you play in your life drama.

This is not another survival book! If you have a roof over your head, clothes on your back and you have enough to eat, compared to millions of people, you are already doing well. This book is about thriving in a life that you are proud of and being the best you can be.

Consider this: A school of thought believes, *"Life lives through each one of us."* I interpret that to mean that we don't live life; *life* lives us. We are all an expression of the life that lives through us. How we think, feel, and interpret that - dictates the life we experience.

For example, If you find it hard to do something that others find easy and you tell yourself that you are useless and a failure, you will tend to avoid other challenges in life for fear of failing. The result is a life of missed opportunities, disappointment, and self-reproach. Alternatively, if you interpret the experience of failing as a challenge to overcome, you respond by improving your skills. Then, your results get better, and your confidence grows. Same experience, alternative perspective.

That leads me to the second part of this book, which focuses on your skills and the process of actively expanding them. Whether that is a hobby or life skill - I put significant importance on getting out of your comfort zone and learning something new or something you have always been interested in or intrigued by - but never explored. The second half of this book will open new worlds and opportunities for you. But only if you follow through and act.

The fact is our environment can hold us back. In the second half of this book, you will learn the difference between your soft and harsh environments and the skills environment you already inhabit. This will open your eyes to all your potential and highlight the pitfalls of staying stuck where you are.

The exciting part is that this is where the rubber meets the road; before the halfway point in this book, you will face the most important vehicle of change – your mindset. Throughout the centuries, philosophers and psychologists have postulated much about the power and potential of the human mind and how little of it we use. I can only relate to my own experience in this area. I originally started to draft this book after working as a volunteer counselor for three years. This experience gave me a huge insight into thought processes. After hundreds of client hours, I coined the phrase 'dysfunctional perspective syndrome' (DPS) to describe the negative behaviors that clients would repeat. From the very start of my counseling training, I disliked the labels that define people. Why? Because people have the fateful habit of living up to their labels. If I use the DPS acronym anywhere else within this book, it means 'Don't Play Stupid.'

At this point in the story, it is worth sharing that the first 30,000-word draft of this book took a 2-year holiday. During this period, I did not write a single word. Not because I was procrastinating or doubted the quality of the content. I simply realized that I needed to step back from it and take a break. Truthfully, I did not give the decision much thought; it felt natural, and I went with my gut instinct.

During this 2-year break, I decided to add a new skill set to my life and career and began my amazing journey into the world of Mindfulness and Hypnotherapy.

Looking back, I have no doubt in my mind that the new understandings and perspectives gained from my studies and private hypnotherapy practice have given me the necessary tools to complete this book finally. Remember what I said about fluidity earlier?

Question: Do you believe that the universe is conspiring to stop you in your tracks and make life difficult for you?

The reality is that the universe is not trying to do anything to you; if life is lived through you, you sabotage your potential for success. If you think honestly about it, you will know this to be true - but accepting it is the hardest challenge. The idea that you could be hampering your own happiness sounds a bit crazy – so look around you and ask yourself, *"How many people do I know that sabotage their lives in some way or another?"* It is ok to accept the fact that we are all capable of doing this. The important thing to be curious about is what causes this to happen to you.

For many people, this is not easy to hear and even harder to accept. We like to think that we are in control. This huge myth needs busting if any progress is to be made. The tools in this book will enable you to regain control by applying conscious effort. It takes discipline, steadfastness, and one's ability to keep going when things get tough.

If you give up at the first hurdle, your chances of success are minimal. But if you keep going, you will learn new lessons and experience new experiences. You will grow.

As one of my greatest teachers once told me, *"There is never nothing going on."* When something holds you back, do not see it as an end in itself – see it as an opportunity. This is your growing edge. Beyond it is a whole new world of experience waiting for you to explore. It will stretch your boundaries and pull you out of your comfort zone.

But before we begin any of this work, let us get one thing straight. There are no original mistakes. The mistakes that you make, that I make, that everyone makes, they have all been made before and they will be made repeatedly. This fact is a great advantage for you because knowing that you cannot make any new mistakes provides you with a sense of connection and camaraderie.

Think about it, how many movies would be released to the public if the directors abandoned each scene after the first 'miss takes?'

If you choose to experience your mistakes as something that confirms how useless, how weak, how pathetic, how lacking, or how poor you are. You deny yourself the opportunity and power to push through all obstacles and problems.

You may think that I'm taking a hard line on people's perceptions and reactions to their mistakes and experiences. I do not doubt that some experiences can be horrific and life changing. I recently watched a TV interview with a war veteran who had lost both legs in an explosion. In that instant, I imagined living without both legs; I felt sick to the stomach. All the limitations flashed through my mind in a millisecond. Then I heard him say how it had improved his life, how he became a para-Olympian and had never felt happier as you are about to discover. Perspective really is everything.

This book draws everything from my own experiences in life. I will rarely go into the finer details but will concentrate on how I cultivated the right mindset and habits to overcome obstacles and achieve success. Read it as you would a story, don't take notes, simply enjoy the ride.

By authoring this book, I am setting myself up to complete a mammoth task, I am holding myself accountable to do what needs to be done to make it available. I am being bold and stepping outside of my comfort zone. Also, deep down inside, I know that it is something I am destined to do.

There is an old saying that I'm unsure of the origin. I've quoted it throughout my life: *"If it's done, it's good."*

Why is it good? Because if it is done, you have moved a step forward and acted, which is good. Once an action is taken, you can move forward from there. You can explore, you can improve, you can adapt, and you can change. This book is all about making change happen.

Let's begin that journey together now…

Chapter 2
The Power of Enthusiasm

In this chapter, I will explore the attitudes and behaviors that drive us forward and give us momentum. I will do this by unpicking those things that have successfully and consistently propelled me toward specific goals during my lifetime.

Firstly, I believe that it all boils down to one thing: I call this my superpower.

That superpower is Enthusiasm. When you explore the origins of the word 'Enthusiasm, ' you'll see references to intense enjoyment, interest, or approval. It *was originally used to refer to a person who was possessed by a god.*

So, how can someone tap into this superpower?

I asked myself this question and began to explore the actions and attitudes I fostered whenever I felt a high degree of enthusiasm for something. The answer was that when I become enthused about something, I have a healthy obsession with it and immerse myself in every detail.

This got me thinking: how can someone instantly adopt the right mental attitude, mind chemistry, or whatever you wish to call it, to tap into this source of power that is essential to make things happen?

The answer lies in recognizing our own patterns of behavior.

Ever since I was young (7 or 8yrs), I was obsessed with angling and constantly daydreamed about my next fishing trip to the local park lake. As a teenager, I remember staying up late, cleaning my floats, and tidying my tacklebox, and I would often sit for hours looking at angling catalogs. One year, I desperately wanted a Mitchell Match fishing reel; it was an incredible innovation with a mechanism enabling me to cast out using just one hand. This object of desire was magical to me, I would sit and stare at the catalogue, at the beautiful new blue fishing reel.

This was well before the internet. The illustrations of that magical fishing reel were a constant reminder of my love for angling. My mum often asked me, *"Kevin (she hated anyone calling me Kev), why are you looking at that catalog again?"* My reply was, *"I'm just imagining owning this reel."* Naturally, she knew this was my subtle way of letting her know what I wanted for Christmas.

After months of obsessing and focusing on that magical fishing reel, I knew I would one day own it.

The good news is, I finally got it, and guess what! It was even better than I imagined. Over the years, I would use that fishing reel with pride, especially during team competitions as a youth and adult at the National Angling Championships when I represented the town where I lived.

There was no doubt I was obsessed with angling.

It is fair to say that this was a healthy obsession; it enriched my life and taught me many things about life and nature. Angling is and always has been my meditation, my focus, and one of my many passions.

This pattern of behavior, of obsessing over something that excites you and moves you forward, is the key ingredient for cultivating enthusiasm.

It is important to recognize the difference between healthy obsessions that fill your life with positive experiences that feel good and unhealthy obsessions that drain your life force and fill your life with negative experiences and things that feel bad.

When I explore the many healthy obsessions I've enjoyed throughout my life, I recognize one behavior that consistently comes up - I always immerse myself in thinking and feeling about it. If I wasn't already doing it and wanted to, I would imagine myself doing it just like I imagined holding that fishing reel.

The truth is that my imagination went way beyond simply holding the fishing reel. I would imagine catching fish using it, reeling them in, and feeling proud. I caught some amazing fish with that reel, and with every fish I caught - I relived the previously imagined experience again because I had already visualized the whole experience of owning the reel, using it, and enjoying the success and pleasure it brought to my life.

The process of immersing myself fully created that healthy obsession that expresses itself to this day as an unwavering and indelible enthusiasm that I believe is part of my DNA.

If you are serious about developing the right mindset, a mindset that is guaranteed to drive you forward with the incredible staying power to overcome your biggest obstacles - you need to develop healthy obsessions.

The great thing about healthy obsessions is they take over small chunks of your life. I am thankful that I have never suffered from mental stress or depression or anything that I would call an unhealthy obsession. Naturally, we all have our ups and downs, and much of 'how we experience life' is down to our perspective. I also appreciate that some of the challenges I have experienced during my lifetime would have been huge challenges for some people and incidental annoyances for others.

This journey begins with healthy obsessions. I believe this is the most effective way to help you move forward and gain momentum. There are lots of ideas and 'paths' to success available to you, and the internet is awash with coaching programs promising to teach you how to realize your goals.

My simple advice to live the life that you want to live, the life that you dream about, is to stop dreaming and start obsessing. Otherwise, you risk being stuck on Groundhog Day when the same thing happens to you repeatedly.

To illustrate the best way to feed your healthy obsession - immersing yourself in the subject or object of your interests, which ultimately manifests as enthusiasm in your life. Is to give an example.

Amongst my many varied healthy obsessions, I love brewing my own beer and cider. Over the years, I have brewed lots of different types and have given a fair share of it away to friends and family. The act of giving and sharing has provided me with some great feedback and a reputation for crafting some 'interesting' brews.

Overall, the pleasure this gives to me encourages me to continue this healthy obsession.

A healthy obsession is much more than a hobby – it becomes an indelible part of your life.

A word of warning here: there is a real chance of becoming a bit of a bore when you have healthy obsessions. And it is especially true that some people do not like people being enthusiastic around them. Maybe because it makes them feel unproductive. I don't really know why, but it is a fact that you'll need to come to terms with; your enthusiasm will be overpowering for some people.

The good news is, when someone else shares your healthy obsession, be prepared for the conversation to go anywhere. Healthy obsessions become a hotbed of conversation and an opportunity to truly connect with others and share knowledge. You will quickly appreciate that you will gain a huge amount of uncommon knowledge with any health obsession. This information does not just go in and sit there, ready for retrieval later. This information becomes an intrinsic part of who you are.

Look back through your life at any healthy obsessions you had or maybe still enjoy. Now, think about the people you know who struggle with addictions or mental health issues. Did these people have healthy obsessions? In my experience, healthy obsessions ward off unhealthy obsessions. Imagine it being like a void that needs filling. If you do not have healthy obsessions, the void can attract unhealthy obsessions or unhealthy habits. Like attracts like, the emptiness soon gets filled with whatever resonates with the attitude and mindset you foster. When you immerse yourself in what you love most, you attract those positive experiences that ward off harmful, life-sucking habits.

Making healthy obsessions and habits a part of your life is important. Get them under your skin. This will give you an incredible amount of energy and resources that you did not even realize you had.

Cultivate the power enthusiasm wherever and whenever you can. Whatever your interests, immerse yourself in that something so thoroughly, so completely that it becomes part of who you are. Being part of who you are does not mean it takes over your life. It is simply one of the many parts that make up your personality. Just because you are passionately interested in and enjoy certain things does not mean that you are living unhealthily; it means that there is a part of you that resonates, appreciates, and enjoys the excitement of having these things in your life.

You already know that I am passionate about my hobbies. Some of my hobbies are a great distraction from my day-to-day work. While other hobbies and interests are intertwined with my work as a Hypnotherapist and Online Marketer – work and interests can flow into each other naturally, becoming part of my signature, my uniqueness.

To be clear, I am not concerned with applying rules to my healthy obsessions; some come and go, and some lay dormant for weeks, months, or even years. I remain curious, I keep an open mind. But most importantly, I keep my mind healthy, with the healthy obsessions that show up in the here and now.

And you can enjoy this too. If you do not recognize any healthy obsessions in your life right now, explore your past, look back over your timeline, and go back to being a child. What did you enjoy obsessing over? What do you consider healthy? I am not talking about what other people would consider healthy, but simply if it brought you pleasure and was not detrimental to your life in any way. Look at it again. Does it still excite you? Are there elements or parts of it that you would like to explore again now, with new, wiser eyes and experience?

When I was younger, some people may have viewed my obsession with angling as a distraction from my schoolwork. I spent my school holidays (and any revision time) on the riverbank as often as possible. Nothing could have swayed me from my passion. Years later, I bought shares and eventually owned an Angling business. This allowed me to travel around the world, attending Angling Exhibitions; I got to meet and work with my angling heroes and was often featured in the angling press. I was living my dream.

Pursuing healthy obsessions can become one of life's most enjoyable and rewarding things.

Chapter 3
The Power of Rituals

It is important to have rituals in your life. These could be as simple as a routine that you follow each day at a certain time. I passionately believe that having routines and rituals that are personal to you - but might not mean anything to anyone else – are essential for gaining structure and discipline in a world that constantly grasps our attention. The fact that some people might think that your rituals are silly is not important. Rituals do not have to have any meaning in the grand scheme of things. But they will mean something to you. I will give you an example.

I often joke that my working week is from Monday to Sunday. Because I love my work, I see each day as work time and playtime and often choose a day in the week to do something else altogether. But whatever the day brings, I always go through my usual routine of washing, dressing, and making breakfast. I have a handful of Brazil nuts and a similar number of dried dates; I add cinnamon and then my homemade Yogurt. Always the same order, dish, and preparation.

I also make myself green tea. I make my green tea with 50/50 loose-leaf green tea and 5/6 jasmine tea pearls. As you can see, there are numerous routines here already. I allow the water in the kettle to settle for three minutes, then I add the water to the teapot. While the tea is infusing, I check if the wood burner ashpan in the house needs emptying. After that, I sit down and eat my breakfast.

At the time of writing, this is the morning ritual I go through every day. Later in the morning, I have another ritual that involves making fresh ground coffee and a glass of filtered water.

As you can see, my morning routine is well-established. Another ritual I have is when I am writing sales copy for my marketing clients. Sometimes, I have hundreds of words to craft into a sales letter or video script. To help me get into 'the writing zone,' I always wear a particular pair of shoes. To some people, this may sound a little crazy. It signifies that I am stepping into the shoes of 'The Copywriter' part of me.

NLP and hypnosis would describe this as 'getting into state', which is a very accurate description of what's happening to my mind when I put on my writing shoes.

My old pair of comfortable/battered suede shoes that lost their laces long ago symbolize something immensely powerful. They also tell me that I am stepping into the customer's shoes, the person I am appealing to through my writing.

Notice how this ritual helps me to focus my attention on purpose. On the one thing I am doing. This ritual pulls everything together to make it very real. I believe it is the sole reason (pun intended) that I never suffer from writer's block.

Once again, ritual and habit give me the momentum and enthusiasm needed to drive forward and keep moving.

Newton's first law states that every object will remain at rest or in uniform motion in a straight line unless compelled to change its state by the action of an external force. I am protecting myself against those external forces by wearing my writing shoes. That is the magic of my writing shoe ritual.

During my morning breakfast routine, I mentioned that I add homemade yogurt. This involves another set of routines outside of the morning schedule. Yoghurt is a cultured product that needs to be prepared and made in batches every 5 days. To most people, this would take up too much time, energy, and effort. Once you embrace the powerful nature of rituals and habits, you'll quickly discover that you have abundant time on your hands to do a host of things that make your life more interesting and exciting. Rituals play an important role in my life, and yet they come effortlessly to me because they all feed into one thing: the dynamics of my purpose.

Look at your life and the ways you could inject some rituals into your daily routine. These will become the driving force behind your motivation and enthusiasm. Choose rituals that you can set up for yourself. You do not have to share them with anyone - they are yours to enjoy and will become part of your own personal signature. By adding these rituals to your life, you are making a personal statement and establishing your intention.

For example, when you associate a particular coat or hat that signifies an action, whatever it is. You are getting into a positive mental state and stamping that moment with your signature.

This behavior will mean much more to you as you continue practicing. Trust me when I tell you that this does not only get you into the right mood, but it also elevates your whole way of thinking. You become energized. I cannot emphasize that enough,

Another huge benefit of getting into this state is your ability to banish other thoughts and distractions. Or, more accurately, the usual mind chatter that can derail you when you are trying to stay focused. These intrusive thoughts cannot break through and come into your mind with any importance once you have entered 'that state.'

Personally, I view this as a form of meditation. Not a sitting down and relaxing type of meditation but a working meditation. Having read what you've read so far, I'm sure you'll agree that it's no coincidence that most religions, cultures, and belief systems - all have very powerful rituals to get their followers into their desired state, be it positive or negative.

I do not doubt that some of those rituals have far wider and greater meanings. What I am speaking about here is creating your own rituals. This is not about religion or any belief system or creed, it is about giving your life its own signature. Your rituals are a powerful confirmation that you are dedicating your time, space, and attitude towards your purpose.

When you focus on building healthy habits and rituals, the unhealthier habits that hinder your progress and happiness will have no room to survive.

Image your mind only has a limited amount of space for habits. If all that space is full of good habits, bad habits will not have space to fill. And now, because your mindset is so strong and so powerful, any weaknesses and vulnerabilities from the past are easily overcome.

Bad habits can often enter our lives at times of great stress. We attract drama and problems and find reasons not to do the things that are important to us, or we abuse our bodies and minds. By practicing our unique good habits and rituals, we create an environment that is not conducive for bad habits to enter and survive. Like you, I can only speak from my own experience. I am not a psychologist or psychiatrist, but I know what works for me. And I know that if it works for me, it can work for you, too.

You may already have your own daily habits or rituals, but maybe you haven't thought about them in the way I'm describing them. To help you emphasize their importance and increase their value, bring them into full awareness and acknowledge for yourself that these rituals are not silly. View them as part of your self-care and self-love. You use them daily; they help protect you and project you toward achieving your goals and dreams.

By now, you may have noticed that I'm repeating my message several times. This is purposeful and designed to help you embed these positive statements in your unconscious mind. You can also help this process along by rereading each chapter. How often have you read a book or watched a film a second time and noticed something completely new? Go back through the last chapter and test that idea now, or come back to read it later and see for yourself. Repetition has great power.

Chapter 4
What Role Do You Play in Your Life Theatre?

In this chapter, I will discuss and explore the roles we all play. Mention role-play to some people, and they shy away, saying, "Oh, *I don't like doing that"*. This may be because they feel uncomfortable or silly. Getting into a different character may take them outside of their comfort zone. We often find it difficult to play the roles we are expected to play every day in life.

Let's explore how strong your present role/s is!

To get started, I want you to imagine a situation; it can be a personal relationship or work situation that you have experienced recently. View yourself within this situation as though it was a soap drama on TV. Look at the different characters within this drama. Who is center stage? Whatever situation you are imagining - look at the finer details. How does the dynamic change when someone new enters the scene? How does each different character change or adapt as the drama unfolds? Does any one-person demand or attract more attention than another? Take a few minutes and observe the whole drama as it unfolds.

Done that? Wonderful... now I want you to reflect on what you saw. Most importantly, I want you to reflect on your role in the drama. How strong was your character compared to others? Did you notice anything interesting about how your role changed as other people came onto the scene or maybe when they spoke in a certain way? Did you find yourself taking a back seat, or did you feel as though you had climbed off the stage and stepped into the audience to become a spectator?

Ok, there is nothing wrong with being a spectator at the right time and in the right place; it can give us an added perspective. But your role is central when it comes down to living your life and driving forward with something you want to achieve. If you feel that you are anywhere other than in the central role of your goals and ambitions - you run the risk of allowing other people to feed off your energy. When this happens, there is much opportunity for distraction and drama. If you recognize that your life is full of drama, stop and observe the part that you play in creating it.

The simple act of stopping and observing is often enough to stop the drama from spreading and, ultimately, derailing your plans.

The fact is any interaction between human beings creates friction, high points, low points, conflict, and pleasure. All these things happen when people come together. Even if you are engaged in a solo project, it will involve other people somehow. We cannot escape our reliance on other people.

How you see yourself in many respects is how the world sees you. How you think and turn up in the world creates your reality.

If you say, *"I'm not good enough"* there's a very good chance that others will join in with the story and confirm that you are not good enough. Everything you think and do creates your reality, and everything you say leaks that reality to the people around you. Trust me, our language communicates much more than the words we speak.

The next time you are in conversation with someone - listen closely to the content of what has been said. Look out for self-deprecating language and absolutes. A great example of self-deprecation is starting a telephone conversation with, *"Hi, it's just me"*. Or absolute language that claims, *"I was never good at sport"*. These unnecessary additions are strewn throughout our language and help us confirm a low opinion of ourselves. In doing so, you are creating your character so others can give you a role based on the information supplied. While all this may initially seem to be going on subconsciously, it soon surfaces and manifests in how others treat you.

Fortunately, there is no getting away from having a role in life, no matter how hard you try - you have a role to play. The best way to handle your role creation is to be mindful of your strengths and be curious about how you can make positive changes in how you turn up in these roles. Essentially, do what you need to do to make your role stronger.

By doing this, I am not suggesting a power struggle. I am talking about being happy within your role in life and within your mind. Not everyone is a natural leader, and not everyone wants to be one. The important thing is to be confident and certain that you are on your own path to purpose.

Have you ever noticed someone doing a menial task or work,

acting like they have the best job in the world? This is what I mean by being in your strongest role in your own mind. It has nothing to do with the perception of others. Read that last sentence again; it has nothing to do with the perception of others.

When you turn up fully for a situation and embrace it, all resistance falls away and makes room for pleasure, peace, and ease.

Remember, you only need to take control of the role you play. Some people will try to control other people's roles to gain an advantage. At a deeper level, this is immoral and unethical. However, there is nothing unethical about owning your space and being fully in your power, and playing your role completely, genuinely, and authentically.

The next time you find yourself in a situation that involves others, try this simple exercise. Begin by observing the different characters within a situation, be playful, and give each character a title or name. You could use the different ranks from the army and assign each person an animal type. Choose the characters/metaphors you feel most familiar or comfortable with. Using character names, animals, or metaphors helps to sort everything out in our minds; metaphors are an excellent way to help our minds make sense of situations and gain a better understanding. Be curious about what you learn from this simple exercise. You may be surprised.

In my work with clients as a hypnotherapist, counsellor, and coach, metaphors are a powerful therapeutic tool. During counseling, I often encourage clients to get creative and choose a new role for themselves. I ask them to tell me about their character's life story. During this role-playing game, clients often amaze themselves at the amount of detail they conjure up to fashion their story.

Some of the stories created during these sessions provide powerful revelations. However, the real value comes from their role in the story. On one occasion, a client shared that their story was making lots of sense and was becoming more meaningful as it unfolded. Moments later, they realized that what they'd shared was something that they couldn't normally express in everyday life. Something that was too painful to share under normal conditions. Stepping outside your story and creating your characters/dynamics can help you see the bigger picture.

To recap:

Choose a recent situation in life and observe the role you played.

Ask yourself, was your role central? were you being authentic and true to yourself? How did others affect your role as the drama played out? What could you change, say, or do in future situations to improve the outcome of your role?

Again, using the information above, observe the situation again, but this time, give all the characters new identities, animal types, or similar. Then, replay the story again as an observer and be interested in how the different characters behave. Are there any subtle changes? Did your role change, and did you gain any insight into your own role in relation to others?

Remember, perception is everything...

Chapter 5
Take a Course and Learn Something New

In this chapter, we'll explore ways for you to expand your experiences and abilities. The best and, by far, the easiest way to do this is to take a short course or buy a kit. Here's an example from my own life: A few years ago, I was gifted a cheese-making kit for my birthday, and as with most gift kits, it sat on the shelf for months.

Then, one rainy weekend, I had some free time to myself and thought, "I'm going to get my cheese-making *kit out and give it a go."* I read the instructions the night before, and it all seemed quite straightforward. The most important thing I remember was ensuring the equipment and work area were clean. It all seemed quite simple. The next morning, after clearing some space in the kitchen, I opened the kit, and after a few hours, things started to come together. Pleased with my progress, I left the cheese curds to drain overnight.

What I witnessed the next morning was magical. It instantly gave me a boost of confidence and a wonderful sense of achievement. From a small cheese-making kit, I'd created delicious soft cheese within 24 hours. It wasn't complicated. It was a simple, biological process. It was something I didn't fully understand, but after using that small gift kit, I went on to buy more cheese-making equipment. Since then, I have made dozens of various types of cheeses: soft cheeses, smelly cheeses, and hard cheeses. I love experimenting with different recipes and regularly give some to family and neighbors to try. It's always a great feeling to get positive feedback.

There are two important things going on here, when applied, that will massively improve your abilities and skills in all areas of your life. When you experience great satisfaction from doing something and you receive feedback from others that your efforts are genuinely appreciated, the feelings of achievement and accomplishment massively feed into your sense of self-worth and feeling valued.

On top of all that positivity, you also expanded your knowledge and skill base.

In the future, whenever a conversation about cheese arises, I'll have more knowledge than the average person. That's a great feeling. It's not a power thing. It's a knowledge thing because I can share that knowledge – after all, I firmly believe that knowledge is a thing to be shared. I can share that knowledge with others, which adds to their understanding and positive perception of me.

Ok, Cheese might not be your thing. I have lots of hobbies, and many of them started off with small kits. I've also taken short courses and different craft courses. During a Willow craft course, I created a willow chicken, a life-size chicken made from willow.

Now, everyone who visits our garden comments on my creation. Perched high on our fence and silhouetted against the sky, he's often mistaken as real. Which always makes me laugh.

Here's the amazing thing that I experienced while attending the willow chicken course. As everyone gathered in the morning and sat around the big round table, we all saw a pile of willow sticks and a beautiful willow-sculptured bird created by the course tutor. I noticed a consistent theme as I listened to the conversations and comments being made. One by one, over 90% of the attendees said to each other, *"I'll never be able to make that."* That's right, before they had even started, they were already discounting themselves. *Sound familiar?*

The tutor was obviously used to this kind of reaction because when someone asked her, *"how many years did it take you to become that good?"* She calmly replied, *"to be honest, you'll all make something as good as this by the end of today."*

Naturally, few of them believed that they could achieve such results. However, by the end of that day, after only 6 hours of being instructed 'how to' - by the skilled tutor. There wasn't a bad example of a willow chicken to be seen.

This proves and goes to show that we can all be guilty of telling ourselves a story that doesn't match our reality. Humans do this all the time. The problem is that this self-defeating activity quickly eats away at our own sense of ability, confidence, and self-worth.

Why do we refuse to give ourselves credit?

The great news is that we can massively improve our self-perception by taking courses like this.

This is very important because: *the world views us how we see ourselves.*

If we tell ourselves that we're no good, we can't do this, or we can't do that, that's how the world will perceive us. Why? because it's consistent with the message we're sending out. What is within us is without. I recall reading, 'If you see somebody dropping litter, it is simply a reflection of their inner life.' Meaning: They have a cluttered mind and lack self-respect. When I read that statement, it immediately made sense to me.

We are all reflections of the stories we tell ourselves and how that makes us feel on the inside, and this is what other people see on the outside. When you attend a course or make a kit, you're re-engineering what is happening on the inside by changing what's happening outside. If you're telling yourself, *"I can't do that, I'm useless, and I don't have the skills."* If you're telling yourself that story but then you force yourself into a situation—for example, you attend a course on how to do something and you discover at the end of that course that you can actually do these things, and quite proficiently too - you come to the realization that you've been living a lie from an inside, outside perspective.

This means that what you've been telling yourself isn't true anymore; you've lifted the curse.

It makes sense. If you produce something at the end of a short course worthy of praise, respect, and admiration, then you can't tell yourself the story that says I'm not creative, artistic, practical, or useless. You can't tell yourself that story anymore because it's inconsistent with reality; it simply isn't true.

Chapter 6
That New Skill Could Change Your Life – It did mine

I started my first business when I was 21. At the time, I was already employed working for the local council as an exhibition designer. The role was mainly graphic design. I created posters and leaflets for local heritage exhibitions. It was a short-term contract for one year, and generally, I was left to my own devices. I really enjoyed the work, and it felt like the ideal job at the time.

While working there, I had the opportunity to attend a short course on screen printing. I knew this would help me to produce larger, high-quality posters for the organization. So, it didn't take much to convince my boss to find the funds to pay for the course.

I thoroughly enjoyed the experience. Apart from being great fun, I also learned many new skills.

Being shown how to do these new things was magical for me. I was buzzing with enthusiasm and excitement and returned to work with a long list of needed materials. Within a couple of weeks, I was mass-producing large posters for our local exhibitions and other venues; word started to spread.

I felt very proud of the work I was creating. A few weeks later, I was approached by a small local clothing manufacturer who wanted to explore short-run printing directly onto fabric.

At the time, punk clothes were very popular. Unusual patterns such as skulls, dogtooth, and paisley patterns were trending. The local company wanted to know if I could help them screen print onto fabric. I'd never done this before but thought that it must be possible. After researching at the local library, the internet wasn't available then, so I put together some ideas to present to the manufacturer.

My plans were accepted, and we decided to try a small project together. After a couple of failed attempts, we managed to print their designs onto fabric successfully. This was exciting. The company was expanding and really wanted to have their own screen-printing facility. That's when they approached me to see if I'd be interested in setting it up for them as a separate business.

I liked the idea; I was only 21, and I was ambitious. I said, *"Yes, let's go for it."*

After securing suitable premises, an old warehouse in the old town area of Kingston Upon Hull. I set out on my printing journey. Word spread fast about our services, and the top London fashion house 'Boy' soon came on board. We also screen-printed original T-shirts that are sold across the world by advertising in music and fashion magazines. Soon, our work was featured in a top alternative fashion magazine. It was all very exciting. But I wanted more. I was ready to expand.

Bearing in mind all this was happening while still working for the local council. Every evening and all my weekends were devoted to this new venture. I was obsessed.

Not satisfied with printing on fabrics, I decided it was time to learn some new skills. I wanted to extend printing onto paper, I wanted to print leaflets, letterheads, and brochures. Customers asked us, *"Can you print onto letters and business cards, can you do all types of printing for us?"*

Again, I did my research and considered the types of machinery needed. I spent hours with the local printer who had been handling all our promotional material. I spent time watching him work and helped him for free in the evenings, and eventually asked if I could buy one of his machines.

He explained that it wasn't like a photocopy; this was a proper printing press that needed a trained operator. I didn't listen to his concerns but was more interested in how quickly it could print paper - it was all very exciting. After some discussions, we finally agreed on a price. Looking back, I agreed to the price to buy machinery that I couldn't operate. The good news is, once it was installed, the printer (who became a good friend) gave me a crash course in Lithographic Printing. Within a week of installing that press, I received my first stationary printing order.

That was the beginning… To cut a long story short, my printing business carried on expanding. Over the years, we added three more presses and other equipment and went on to print everything from books to brochures for hundreds of customers.

Over a 12-year period, we employed over 100 people - *and it all began with a weekend course on screen printing at our local community center.*

As you can see, a new skill can dramatically change your life.

I have always loved the phrase – *'the illusion of technique'*. Having a method from which you can create something gives the illusion that you are very skilled. We can all discover techniques that make us look amazing. It's true; learning a technique gives you the skills to achieve great things, and anyone can learn a skill. You can amaze yourself, and you can amaze other people, too. Take those courses. Do the work. Learn new skills. Expand your mind and expand your experience. Expand your life.

I promise you will receive far more than it will ever cost you to do these things. It will also massively improve your self-esteem and your confidence. Just do it. Don't put it off. Don't say, *"I was thinking of..."* because thinking alone doesn't create things. Don't say, *"I'd love to do that, but..."* Don't put a 'but' in there. The only butt you should have in this world is the one that you sit on. Do it. Enroll on a course/s, take the plunge.

Over the years, I've heard many stories of people who had a chance to meet, have taken a course, met someone new, and their world has expanded exponentially. They couldn't even start to imagine the opportunities that have opened for them. Take a course; don't sit at home, thinking of all the things you're going to do and not actually doing them. Just do it. Take the plunge.

OK, imagine you have a spare £50, you have a choice, do you go for a meal, do you buy yourself new clothes? These are transient things. The moment you buy them, the experience starts to slowly fade. However, buying a training course could change the direction of your life. Remember, it doesn't always have to be something that's in your comfort zone. You know I like arts and crafts, yet a close family member bought me a cheese kit. I wouldn't have chosen it because it was outside my comfort zone.

The cheese-making kit changed my life in many ways. I now love making and eating different cheeses and sharing them with friends. When I get feedback, it helps me to improve my skills and encourages me to try new recipes. It also expands your conversational repertoire as well. When people are interested in what you do, they see you as an interesting person. That's a great attribute. When someone says, *"I was talking so and so, they're really interesting"*. It shows that they were interested and that you got their attention.

Think of all the positive ways that this quality can help you in your work and relationships.

Getting people's attention is hard these days. Expanding your knowledge and being able to talk about something with a degree of authority demonstrates that you are a resourceful person. Resourceful people get more resources. That is the law of the jungle.

People are often amazed to hear that a small round of cheese takes 10 liters of milk to make. They comment, *"That's an awful lot of waste. What do you do with the other 9 liters?"* I explain that the other 9 liters (the whey) have many uses, that I add it to my water barrels for the greenhouse, mix it 50/50 with water and salt to preserve vegetables, and make sauerkraut. This opens a whole range of opportunities and ideas which might save you money, give you other interests or take you in a new direction.

Take a course. Change the course of your life. I know that my life is far richer from having all those experiences. It fills me with satisfaction. Being satisfied with what I achieve and do is a great motivating force and helps drive me forward.

What's this got to do with NEVER GIVING UP?... Everything! You must persevere whenever you take on a new project that takes you out of your comfort zone. You must push forward. You must take on board new instructions, new models, new ideas, and new processes. You may not be sure at first and question your abilities; it's natural. Persevere with it. Push forward. See what happens and be curious. Never Give Up!

Curiosity, enthusiasm, energy, and interest - will massively expand your life and your mind. For me, this is the true route of happiness. If someone were to ask me now, *"How do you rate your happiness on a scale of one to ten?"* It's a ten. It's been a ten for a long time. Why? Because I know that I consistently contribute to it. I feed that happiness with my actions. I don't wait for somebody else or something to make me happy.

A Note about happiness:

We've all heard people say, "He or She makes me feel so happy."

They get their sense of happiness from an external source. Is that true happiness? No, that happiness is transient; it's something that can and often will pass. When the other person does something to make them feel unhappy or isn't in their life anymore, they change their statement to, *"They made me feel so unhappy"*. But that's impossible because they wouldn't be happy in the first place if they relied on another person to make them happy.

In truth, the person who left them left them the way they found them, unhappy.

Can you see what a huge responsibility humans put on the shoulders of others?

People in our lives may contribute to our existing level of happiness, but they aren't in control of our overall happiness.

Think about the way you talk about where happiness comes from.

Chapter 7
Why Perfectionism is the End of Progress

Perfectionism is yet another obstacle that damages your chances of success. That may sound like an oxymoron, but it's true. Perfectionism is such an extreme standard that those afflicted, or perfectionists as we know them, rarely get started on any project. It makes sense when you think about why someone would start a project if the circumstances weren't perfect? Why would anyone set themselves up to fail?

Ask yourself this, *"Are perfectionists more committed to failing or succeeding?"*

If you're a perfectionist or like to think of yourself as a perfectionist - you've probably never failed or committed yourself to anything wholeheartedly.

Why? Because the risk far outweighed the gain – or so you thought!

Take this book for instance. I accept that it is far from perfect;

my grammar has never been great, and structurally, I'm probably way off the mark. But that's not why I wrote it. I didn't write this book to win literary awards – I wrote it to share my practical understanding and experiences of Never Giving Up.

From the start, my intention was clear: to share my experiences using the medium of a traditional book. I also intend to make it available as a Kindle and audiobook.

I didn't look for the perfect timing or situation. I had a simple idea, gave myself some milestones, and made a start.

The problem with being a perfectionist is that it gives you a great reason, sorry… a great excuse to do nothing. When we procrastinate about the things we're doing. It's as though we're doing some important work, using up lots of energy, and achieving nothing. Of course, we're not doing work really. We're not moving forward with the project; we're simply treading water. Talking a good fight, convincing, and conning ourselves and the people around us that everything will fall into place when the time is right.

But this goes against Newton's first law of motion or the law of inertia – *"An object at rest stays at rest, and an object in motion stays in motion with the same speed and in the same direction unless acted upon by an unbalanced force."*

If you're a pioneer, like many entrepreneurs past and present, you're willing to put one foot in front of the other into the unknown. Even if only to test the ground, see what happens, and get feedback.

Never Giving Up relies on a healthy level of curiosity, which is healthy, playful, and childlike. On the other hand, when you want everything to be just perfect, you want the impossible.

NEVER GIVE UP

When a client exclaims, *"I can't do that because it's impossible,"* I help them rephrase it using a word that's more open to possibilities. The word is improbable.

This small change often makes a big enough shift to allow them to take the first step.

When you make the first step, the next step follows straight in front of you and you're moving forward. When you want everything to be perfect, you're standing still. You're not moving towards the future; you are living in the future. You're living in a future that doesn't exist, but it does exist in your mind as an unhappy thought.

Look at it this way: by being a perfectionist, you're not allowing the future to unfold. You want the future to be just so. You want the future to be just as you imagined. You want the future to be ideal.

Truthfully, there's no ideal future because so many things affect our lives, our circumstances, everything from our health, work, money, and our families. There are so many things impacting our lives at any one time that we cannot even start to imagine the implications and complexities of how each one affects us. Within all this confusion and fear of the unknown – the perfectionist steps outside of reality, creates an image of the future, and then defends it with their life.

OK, that may sound extreme, but in many ways, it's true. Defending our right to be right has become a common psychosis these days.

The Danish have a word for it: 'Hygge'

Hygge - *"A quality of coziness and comfortable conviviality that engenders a feeling of contentment or well-being."*

A couple of years ago, I spent a long weekend with my extended family. We sat around talking and had a lovely campfire going on a beautiful summer evening. We got onto the subject of different lifestyles. Some of our relatives work in London, work very long hours and spend a long-time commuting. I was shocked to hear them say how they don't even live for their weekends anymore. Their weekends are rushed, there's no time to relax or cook meals, they're even buying pre-prepared food. I asked why, and they said that when the weekend comes around, they're already exhausted and lack energy. They do try to make the most of the weekends but usually only really get to relax and enjoy their vacation times.

Neither of these people were happy about their situation. Then, I noticed one comment from the conversation that really stood out for me. That was that we. My partner and I are *"some of the lucky ones."* They commented on us having the ideal lifestyle, which is more relaxed, working from home, and enjoying hobbies. I was shocked that they thought our lifestyle had something to do with luck.

That got me thinking: did they feel unlucky by comparison?

Was our life situation out of reach for them?

Did they imagine that things were perfect for us?

If they could have this type of lifestyle, have enough money to enjoy life without working long hours… and have the time and the freedom. Would they really be happy?

Then it dawned on me - if they consider us the 'lucky ones', our lifestyle would always be out of their reach.

As you read this, this might not be obvious to you – allow me to explain. None of this, our choices, plans or lifestyle, has come about through luck. It has come from hard work, from being willing to take risks; it's happened by putting one foot in front of the other and persevering. And trust me, there's no amount of perfectionism in any of it. If we had waited for the 'right time,' we would still be waiting, waiting, and hoping to get lucky.

I learned from my mistakes. NO, scrap that...I enjoyed my mistakes. As crazy as that may sound. Some of the best things that have happened to me would be considered life-crushing catastrophes by most people. Why? Because it's all about perspective. When you denounce perfectionism, as I do. When you realize that perfectionism is the 'one thing' that holds people back, far more than poor self-belief. Even when you have a strong sense of self-worth, great competence, and unshakable confidence, even when you trust in your own abilities when others doubt you, perfectionism will still creep in through the back door and sabotage your plans.

Imagine several opportunities laid out before you that you don't take - because you're being hijacked by your attitude of wanting things to be perfect. Your self-talk demands that the timing must be perfect, the situation should be perfect, and your bank balance must be perfect. These are not reasons - but excuses. The most important thing is adopting the right attitude and having the courage to take that first step. Ok, just because you take one first step forward doesn't mean that you must take the second or third. You may pull back after the first step and regroup your thoughts and ideas.

Taking the first always opens new horizons; you get one step closer and discover something new. The new discovery automatically gets added to your awareness and knowledge base, and you adjust your plans accordingly. This step-by-step approach is not just a metaphor for taking small bites at a time. The process of taking one step gets you in motion.

When thinking about taking the first step, most people face the problem is imagining the outcome. For some reason, they think that committing to that first step is like bungee jumping without a rope. They lose their options and enter a no-turning-back scenario. The great news is you do have options. Just because you take the first step doesn't mean you're on a roller coaster ride into the unknown. Of course, It can be frightening to step outside of the norm, but more importantly, it's crucial for you to be a pioneer in your own life. It's important to step out and explore new lands because they're your lands. They're your experiences to enjoy, and they will never be perfect. Nothing will ever be perfectly as you imagine them to be – but you will get some pleasant surprises along the way, and trust me when I say, *"Things will be even better than you ever imagined perfect could be."*

Review your life experiences and find a time or situation that now looks perfect to you. On reflection and looking back, we all say things like, *"That holiday was perfect, the weather, the food, the company, the traveling. It was all just perfect."*. Memories have that special quality because they are wrapped up neatly within our perspective blanket. On the other hand, when we project perfectionism into the future, we create a false ideal that loses all sense of perspective because it's an illusion and not a concrete memory. All it will do is rob you of the opportunity to live a rich and meaningful life.

Take the first step and see for yourself.

One foot forward, explore, be curious, and enjoy the experience.

Chapter 8
How Your Soft Environment Defines You

What is the best environment for persevering? What is the best environment for pushing forward and making things happen in a positive way? On a personal level, I had to do a lot of work on my soft environment before I could start to get solid results and get a true sense that I was on track. Where I lived, my relationships, the people, and the things I had around me – all got audited. Your soft environment includes the people in your life. Your hard environment is the physicality of where you live, and the skills environment includes the tools you use to make things happen. All these environments impact on your ability to win - through thick and thin.

Let's look at people to start with. Are there people in your life that you feel hold you back? Are there people in your life that give you positive praise? Are there people who take more than they contribute?

Maybe it's time to look hard at this area of your life and do what

I call a friendship audit'. Initially, this might sound very harsh and clinical. But this is massively important - we're talking about the health of your life because your environmental and mental health does, in many ways, rely on the people that you surround yourself with.

The famous writer and motivational genius Earl Nightingale said, *"You become an average of the people we surround ourselves with."*

On a sliding scale of one to ten, imagine all the people you surround yourself with and how great their lives are. Where do you sit on that scale? Are you happy with that average? Could reducing the amount of time you spend with certain people increase your average by a few points? Try it, I guarantee it will have a positive impact on all parts of your life. It will also allow you to spend more time with the people higher up on the scale. How would that feel?

Let me clarify one thing… I'm not talking about blaming the people in your life for holding you back. This isn't a blame game. This is all about taking stock. This is about taking an audit of your life. Where certain things can be changed. And yes, it takes a lot of courage to cut off connections with some people altogether. You know who they are, they know who they are, and you've tolerated them long enough.

Years ago, I employed a sales representative in my printing business. He said all the right things, looked the part, and made some great appointments with prospective clients. The problem was that he wasn't closing any deals. Every day, he'd hand my secretary a list of his appointments, and every evening, he'd come back to the office to do his paperwork. After a week of making calls, I approached him to see how things were going. At this point, he confessed to only going after bigger deals than the other reps because he wanted to earn higher commissions. At this point, his sales were zero. I explained that new customers would usually place a small order to test our delivery and quality, and only then would they place bigger orders. He agreed and spent another week failing to close a deal. Again, I asked how things were going. This time, he said he'd taken my advice but decided to only approach large organizations because even their smallest order would be bigger than anything the other reps were pulling in.

At this point, I could see he was a wildcard type of character and suggested that he tried to pull in at least one order – no matter how small- to establish himself with a client. You guessed it, a week later he hadn't made a sale and came up with yet another reason (excuse). At this point, I said that I'd have to let him go and wished him luck what he said next stuck with me forever. He looked at me and smiled, and said, "I'm surprised you let me stay so long".

Could that be happening to you? Could someone be hanging around, taking more than they contribute to your life, and wondering how long you'll tolerate them for? Maybe it's time to let them go; they're probably expecting it.

You may be thinking, that seems tough. Test it, spend a little less time with someone who takes more, and experience the difference. I'm not suggesting that you behave mean to anybody. I'm talking about making a conscious choice. I'm talking about making a positive statement in your life. It's a fact of life that some people take more than they give. That's how they get by and you find yourself pandering to their needs and compensating for their shortcomings. Maybe you're trying to rescue them. Maybe you have a personal mission to help others at the expense of your own happiness, whether conscious or unconscious.

The truth is you can't save anybody. Everyone has their course to take. Everyone has a road that they need to walk on. And it's not your responsibility to save them. In my own experience, whenever I've tried to save someone from themselves, it becomes a huge distraction from taking care of myself. After lots of inner reflection and therapy, I realized that I didn't feel worthy of looking after myself. So, I gave that attention, that love, to someone else. I projected it onto someone else instead of myself.

"Charity begins at home."

Take a good look at your relationships and ask yourself, am I projecting the attention I should give myself onto someone else? This is not about whether the other person is deserving or worthy, and it's not about making judgments. This is about being honest. Being authentic to yourself, to your own needs. Look at the people you surround yourself with. It may be friends, it might be relationships, it might be family. Be honest and look at what changes you would like to make. Maybe you choose to spend less time or energy on them.

It's important to measure these changes' impact because we can only change what we measure. Maybe it allows you more time to concentrate on the projects that you've been putting off or a new course you want to pursue.

Look, I get it, it's okay to like the feeling of being needed. Everyone likes to feel needed. Yet sometimes it can become a burden, and sometimes it can be a massive distraction from getting on with our own stuff. When our need to be needed becomes greater than our need to progress with a project we're passionate about, there can be only one outcome. At some level, resentment will replace our goodwill and intention, and we'll have conflicts with ourselves.

I call this the long way around – continuing with this kind of dysfunctional behavior will end with you self-sabotaging the need to be liked or wanted. What happens is this: our wiser self creates situations and feelings that enable our greater need to progress in life - to shine through. So, as you can see, I'm not talking about being cruel to anyone. I'm not talking about cutting everybody off and becoming a recluse. I'm saying, *"identify where you can make some small changes because these can have a big impact on your life."*

Often, making a small behavior change with the people that you surround yourself with can have a disproportional knock-on effect. Observe the areas of your life that might not have been going so well and see how they quickly start to improve.

When there's a small shift, look closely and observe the changes. Be curious about what they represent and the opportunities and possibilities they open within your life.

Chapter 9
Your Hard Environment Refines You

The second type of environment is where you live. Think of it as the roof over your head. How does that environment impact your happiness and the energy that you need to push forward? Sometimes, environments can be perfect for our needs. They can be perfect for our well-being, healthiness, and sense of peace. A simple example is the amount of light that comes into your home or the types of noise pollution that invade your space. Everything affects us in some small way, and all things in our hard environment impact our ability to concentrate.

That's why it's important to prepare and set up the right environment. I'm not just talking about when you sit down for work. It's common for people to set up the right mood and space when they're writing or studying something. They make time and space special. But this is NOT what I'm talking about. What I'm referring to is your living environment in general, always.

What changes can you make to your environment, and how can

you make sure these changes align with how you choose to live 100% of the time - not just 'special times'? These changes are more in line with your life preferences, more in line with your positive choice to make change happen, and less to do with quality time. There is a huge difference.

Imagine you're writing a book and you're living above a bar, but you like to write at night. That environment may not be conducive for someone who likes to work in peace and quiet. On the other hand, some people like noise and lots of activity in the background, so it feels perfect for them.

My point is environmental conditions are a very personal thing. It's not something that's 'one-size fits all'. Remember, the environment is very personal to you; it is an extension of you. The things around you, the physical things around you that influence you, must be aligned with who you are, or they will conflict and disrupt.

We've all heard people say, "I'll get on with that project, or I'll write that book, or I'll start that business when I move house or when I go on holiday." The holiday example is perfect. Here's why…

Going on vacation is a perfect way of shifting your environment. Even though it's usually short-lived, vacations are a great way to shift your gears up a notch and put you in a different state of mind. This puts you in a different place physically, emotionally, and mentally.

The great news is your everyday environment can have that quality, too.

Even in the so-called 'civilized world', people live in terribly unhealthy environments. Modern lifestyles are insane, and people suffer stress at every level of existence. Since the industrial revolution, everything seems to be shifting, with humans becoming like robots. Operating on a level of 'system overload' to maximize productivity to satisfy the cancer of consumerism.

We buy the latest car, a house that's way too big with an even heftier mortgage, buy bigger and better TVs, travel long distances to work, and spend more time commuting than reading or relaxing.

The commuting environment is super stressful. Cancelled trains and traffic jams, hemmed in like cattle. What part of that is healthy?

There's a reason why they call it the rat race.

Whenever I drive into the city, I look at the faces of people in cars. I wonder where they are - none of them look present. They're trapped in an environment that they don't wish to be in. In an anxious state of stress, they drift off somewhere else, possibly worrying about their next mortgage payment possibly worrying about their relationship because they hardly ever see each other.

Think about the hard environments that surround you.

Think about what you can change to improve those environments. In recent years, many people are getting permission, in some cases actively being encouraged, to work from home. This is a great way of leveraging technology to build positive lifestyles. It makes sense that people want to spend more time in the home they spend a fortune on. Working virtually may still be in its infancy, but it will massively impact our working habits in the future. Imagine enjoying your home more, spending less time travelling to work, and all the added benefits that will bring.

What's the point in working all hours, spending huge amounts of time commuting, to only spend a few hours asleep in the house that you've aspired to? It's insanity. Think about the things you do right now that seem slightly insane. Imagine an alien visiting Earth for the first time, watching the behaviors of the masses. Would they think, Hmmm, this is all very harmonious, happy, and positive!

Or would they think… Humans are crazy!

Look at your environment and make some positive changes. Do you really need that fuel-guzzling car? Could you or your ego cope with something smaller, more efficient? What would you do with all the money you'd save? Maybe you could afford another holiday to get even more inspiration? Holidays are a great way to get inspired. But you need to keep that momentum once you get home again. The idea is to make your whole life a big adventure and stay constantly inspired.

That's a big deal, and it's something I'm personally working on right now, something I'm striving towards with every thought and action. The great thing for me is it's working. Look at your environment, look at what changes you can make, and make some small changes today. It doesn't matter how small those changes are. Remember that everything is relevant, but not everything is relative. Sometimes, a small change can have a huge impact, and a big change can have a small impact.

Consider this: there's no scale to measure this by, and there's no sense in any of this. If you're looking for a logical answer to all this, you will be disappointed. Simply make those changes, be curious, and observe the outcomes. That's proof enough.

NEVER GIVE UP

When you contribute positively to your life, life pays you back. Life rewards you for doing something for you. It's like you're connecting with a part of you that acknowledges the attention and gives thanks. The giving of thanks can come in many ways. Some people might say it's good fortune shining on you. Or maybe it's a direct result of your actions that allow positive alignments to give you more of your needs. Maybe it's because you're taking control and doing something positive for yourself for once.

Changing your environment could include painting a wall a different color. Maybe the previous tenant painted the house you rented in heavy, oppressive colors. Just Do it. Make those small changes. Never underestimate the impact that small changes can have on your life. Improve your environment. Improve your lifestyle in positive ways. Make it your mantra, your discipline.

What can I change to make my environment better? Ask yourself this question. How can I create a more positive environment for myself?

Unfortunately, if you're the type of person who sits back and says, *"It's not my fault, I have to do this job in order to pay for my big mortgage and my expensive new car, plus my boss expects me to work 70 hours a week because everyone else in the office does"* My reply would be, *"stop whining"* You got yourself into this mess and the good news is, you can get yourself out of this mess by making small, positive changes.

It's a fact of life that one day, we all die, and no one knows when their final day will be.

I read a story about a journalist who interviewed a group of people about the things they regretted most in their life. The defining part of this line of questioning was that these people in a hospice didn't have long to live. Imagine being asked that question when you know that life is about to end for you. What aspects of your life would you regret? Without being in their situation, I imagine it's hard to be 100% honest. However, they unanimously said that they regretted the things they hadn't done, not the things they had. Think about that for a moment. They regretted the things they didn't do.

Could this be because we're all so scared about regretting what we do - that we paralyze our future and avoid acting?

Goethe sums this up perfectly when he has Faust speak these lines to Mephistopheles:

"Where I to say the pleasing present should remain, and that is what I truly meant… Then you may throw me into chains, And I will gladly seal my doom."

Chapter 10
Your Skills and Tools Environment Enables You

The third and final environment houses our tools. Everything we use to get us where we need to be. This could be a motor vehicle, or it may be a laptop, microphone, or webcam. Whatever equipment you use to get you where you want to be. This is your tools environment. Like all environments, this space needs to be finely tuned and effective. This means that everything you use to help you on your journey needs to be of a high quality.

It needs to be reliable because of one very important reason.

Anything that lets you down is another excuse for not getting things done.

If your vehicle doesn't work properly, it lets you down, and it lets your project down. When I say 'vehicle', I mean anything that helps you get the job done or gives you momentum. Here's an example from my life: When I first started working online, I did voiceover work for Explainer videos. I quickly discovered that the quality of audio I was turning out was below the expected standard. So, I decided to invest in a studio-quality microphone. Initially, I did my homework by researching audio forums and review sites. The great thing about researching products is the huge amount of information available. There's no excuse for failing to apply due diligence and getting properly informed about the best equipment for the job. There are people everywhere on the internet who are willing to share information and their review videos on YouTube and blogs.

It makes sense to be cautious with some review blogs and not immediately take their word as gospel. Many review sites are retail pages posing as review sites and are packed with affiliate links. The truth is, many of these sites are only interested in your money and not the information they share. When I suggest doing some due diligence, I genuinely mean that you need to to spend enough time to get the best picture and read up about the items you want to buy.

The biggest thing I've learned about buying equipment is not buying cheap. When you buy cheap equipment, you don't buy it once; you end up paying repeatedly. It will cost you more in the long run and also damage your reputation. Because you're in this for the long haul, cheap will only give you one thing. Constant pain. In direct contrast to this, buying something that's high quality may initially hurt your wallet, but over the years you come to appreciate it as an investment in you. When you reflect on what a great buy that was and talk about how reliable it is and what great jobs it's done. You feel good about the choices you make.

From the minute you buy it (apart from the short-lived pain of that initial purchase) until its natural life ends – you feel happy with your choice. But when you buy something cheap, you enjoy it the first day you buy it because you think, wow, I got a bargain! And then you regret it forevermore. Look at the contrast here. Initially, with the expensive item, it hurt at first. But you felt proud about telling people, yeah, I've bought a top-of-the-range microphone—well, only the best to get the best job done, eh! you feel proud about the experience. You feel it inside as a personal achievement. On the flip side, when you buy cheap and look at your crappy microphone that does a poor job, there's nothing to boast about, and every time you do a job, it lets you down.

Think about all the vehicles you use to get the job done. The things that help you achieve what you want to achieve. As I mentioned earlier in this chapter, some people will use this as an excuse. They claim that they didn't do a very good job because this or that equipment let them down. Truth is, this isn't a valid reason at all. They are making excuses. The real reason they didn't do a very good job is because they bought cheap. They cut corners. Don't cut corners. When you put your mind to something, be a square!

I made a list when I started buying equipment for my online marketing business. I listed everything I needed to provide a solid quality service. After researching the best microphone for the job, I saved up until I could afford it. At the time, my income was minimal, and it took a few months. When the parcel arrived, I opened the box and experienced great achievement. The next item on my list was a good-quality webcam. Having a good-quality webcam was important to me at the time because I wanted to keep my customers happy. I invested in the best that I could afford. Again, it took a few weeks to save the money, but then I had the two most important items I needed.

The next step was building a small audio booth to cut out the background noise. At the time, I lived in a noisy neighborhood. I wouldn't know if someone would be cutting the grass or if people would be talking in their gardens. I needed to be able to cut out the background noise whenever I wanted. OK, you may be wondering, how does all this tie in with perseverance and never giving up? The simple answer is that if you don't get your environment right, you're allowing external things to sabotage your progress.

I cannot stress this enough. When you get everything in balance, remember, I'm not suggesting that you must get everything perfect- because, as you know, that's another way of setting yourself up to fail. What I'm suggesting is if you get things right you make sure you pay attention to detail, and apply a craftsmanship attitude to what you do, people are going to notice. When you get your tools environment right, you know that you will be heard and seen clearly. And more importantly, you will be respected as a person who takes their work seriously.

Chapter 11
Getting Your Mindset Aligned

In this chapter, I will talk about something that's probably the most important part of this book. That is - getting your psychology right. What do I mean by getting your psychology right? First, let's establish a baseline for this chapter. Irrespective of what psychologists tell us about how easy or how hard it is to affect someone's attitude toward things. We are all affected by internal and external forces 24/7. These sources of influence are constantly at play no matter what we're doing.

One of the only times that internal forces aren't at play within our psychology is when we are sitting calmly in a meditative state. Other than that, there's always something going on in our heads. To test this, stop reading or listening to this book, stop for a moment, and watch the activity of your mind.

Observe your thoughts as a third party looking in and see what comes up. Once a thought comes into your mind, the next thing that happens is another thought that attaches it to the first thought.

What you experience is a stream of thought. I call these streams 'thought forms' and you'll find them flowing through your mind all day. Normally, these thought forms happen unconsciously because we're not aware of them all the time. Can you imagine living with this constant chatter in your head? I know what you're thinking: your head would explode. But the truth is, this activity happens all the time, and It's very rare that our minds are quiet.

What can we do about this noise?

You may decide to become a Buddhist and meditate for hours a day. For most people, this would be an extreme course of action. The good news is you can do things to help calm your mind. I'm not a big fan of going on retreats or visiting spiritual places. When people say, *"I'm going to discover my spirituality and travel all the way to India."* It makes me laugh. I find this notion crazy because they're saying that spirituality can be found or exists in a physical place.

OK, maybe I'm being a bit harsh when I say, 'It makes me laugh.' I have never been to India or any spiritual centers around the world, but I'm sure these places have a powerful influence on people. I'm saying, "I don't believe a place can give you any more spirituality or *sense of peace than where you are right now."* How can that be? Wherever you are, that's where you are. You're right here in this present moment. If you are in this moment, and your mind is full of chatter, full of those constant streams of thought forms with an irrepressible amount of information coming in. It doesn't matter whether you're here, there, or in the most spiritual place on top of a mountain.

The fact remains that you are still exactly where you are in your head.

Here's what you can do to reduce your life's constant internal noise or mind drama.

First, let's talk about the type of TV programs and films you watch. If you're the type of person who likes to watch soaps and reality TV programs - observe what's happening while you're watching these monstrous things. We allow the script on the TV to replace the constant chatter in our minds. This escapism gives us some short-lived relief from our mind-drama but always leaves us wanting more. The problem with this type of stimulation is it's like an addiction. We replace one negative thing with another, and the cycle continues.

But there's a more sinister side to this reality-based program that few people care to accept or admit. All the time you're switched off in your head and into the TV, you're absorbing all the stress and beliefs these programs present. In short, you are in a mental state that makes you highly open to suggestions. This hypnotic state allows information to flow unhindered and unquestioned.

I don't expect everyone to share my views on this but hear me out.

Some people will argue that soaps are simply a reflection of society, are purely for entertainment, and are perfectly harmless. But what if we flipped that notion completely on its head? What if society becomes a reflection of the soap dramas on mainstream TV? What if these seemingly innocent vignettes of society are fashioning life as we know it? Personally, I think this is very real. The aptly named 'reality TV' is more about changing reality and less about reflecting it.

Dramas, soap operas, and even nature programs are all starting to follow a set pattern. Instead of reflecting society and the reality of life in its many mundane forms. Producers and writers must inject energy and stress to make it exciting and get us to come back for more. To do this effectively, they have to distill the content. In one episode, in one half-hour episode, there could be a murder, a birth, a death, someone will be having an affair, and someone will have cancer diagnosed. I accept that all these things do happen in real life. But at a much more diluted pace.

When we are exposed to these stressors and when we are in a super suggestible state. Image the impact on our mental wellbeing.

By watching these programs, you're absorbing super-concentrated external stressors.

Seriously, I am 100% suggesting that watching TV is stressful. Now, you might object and call me a crazy person and argue that watching these programs makes you feel lucky that your life isn't that way.

NOT YET AT LEAST!

I'd say that your life will become more and more that way if you expose yourself to these dramas. This constant barrage of 'super-reality' plays with your mind insidiously by exaggerating and concentrating on the negative aspects of human behavior.

The problem is good news doesn't sell. Bad news sells. Look at the headlines in most mainstream newspapers; you'll see evidence of this every day of the week. This brings me to another great way of reducing the amount of stress and the amount of trauma in your life - avoid the tabloid newspapers. You may argue, yeah, but I won't get any news or current affairs, I won't keep up with what's happening in the world if you believe that you've already bought into the illusion that the tabloids sell news. Newspapers would have gone out of business long ago if they served real news. The truth about what's going on, even in your own city, is rarely presented on the front page of any newspaper. Newspapers are in the business of distorting the news to make it look sensational and attractive.

Let me clarify something very important before you start getting angry at the press. I'm not suggesting that the newspapers are playing the conspiracy game (OK, MAYBE THEY DO THAT TO). They simply give the public what the public wants and needs. They'd go out of business if they didn't satisfy this ever-growing demand for dramatized news.

The good news is that there are places where you can find some genuine news if you take the time to look for it. I won't recommend any sites or publications here – do your homework and make your mind up. Just remember, buying what's often referred to as the gutter press, daily newspapers, and tabloids won't give you the down-to-earth boring news; they'll give you a version geared to dramatize life and the society that we live in and help to promote the consumerism that we all buy into when we choose to not think for ourselves and make considered choices.

Most people in the Western world are suckers for a distressing story. If you've ever seen the film. The Shipping News. Newbie Quoyle lands a new job as a journalist with the local rag, and a colleague explains that he needs to cover local car crashes because bad news sells newspapers. Then, he receives specific instructions about how to photograph the car crash. More specifically, he's told to carefully place a child's shoe in the grass in the main photo. He realizes that all this is done to build a picture in the reader's mind of what could have happened; it draws the reader in and enables them to fill in the pieces for themselves – before they've bought the newspaper. But now, with a mental picture already forming, they want to know all the details of the dramatic story.

All this drama exaggerates life and can potentially do a lot of mental and emotional damage. Managing your psychology is very important if you want to persevere, push forward with projects and make positive changes in your life. Drama distracts you from real work. If anything, it's escapism. You're escaping from the present moment, where you have very few problems, and you're stepping into an imagined realm that relies on you to fill in the blanks based on the information given.

I've got nothing against escapism. What's important is that the amount you consume needs to be balanced with the amount of quiet, calm reflection and relaxation you have in your life.

There's no 'one rule fits all' when it comes to getting yourself into a positive state. People who do creative work might choose to listen to inspiring music to help them relax and come up with new groundbreaking ideas - while others get together and brainstorm in a more active/creative environment. Both apply a simple rule: when you shut out the distractions of life, you enter a different state of mind that's more conducive to thinking clearly and creatively. You don't need to be an artist or executive to do this - you can do it yourself by finding ways of shutting out the distractions and reducing the amount of artificial drama that you consume.

Maybe you have someone in your life that brings drama to every situation. I'm certain that everyone knows someone like that. They could be constantly in and out of relationships and reliving the same old stories and behaviors. There's always a reason why they do that, there's a reason why they repeat the same life story repeatedly.

Some people feel safe and comfortable on familiar ground. Or maybe they believe that they don't deserve better. This is their stuff. Their stuff that they're adding onto their life story, onto their drama.

Whoever it is, friends, family, or close relationships. It feels like they're plowing the same old furrow in the field of their existence. Nothing seems to shift them from the drama mindset, from the pattern of behavior that confirms their destructive beliefs. The most important thing to remember is this – *"You're not here to rescue them and make everything OK again."* That is not your responsibility and role in life – you have your own path, and they have their own journey to take.

If you have someone like this in your life and they are negatively impacting your mental well-being, you simply need to reduce your exposure to that person. That may sound harsh uncaring and brutal. But It's a fact that will liberate you from more drama and put you in a much better position to help people from a position of strength instead of a positive mental weakness.

If a person in your life constantly comes demanding your attention because of a repeated life drama, you need to know when to say NO. You need to know when to turn yourself away from all that exposure.

Truth is… on many levels, no matter what you might think you can do to help them - they feed it constantly to keep it alive. Try your conscious best to distance yourself from that kind of drama in life. Otherwise, it will sabotage the amount of time and quality of energy that you'd like to put into your projects. This type of drama will eat away at the roots of your discipline and routine and, ultimately - at your ability to persevere. Even the subtlest of disruptions, caused by this mental and emotional spinning top - will eat away at your ability to perform at optimum levels of productivity and reduce your physical and mental strength.

Be mindful. Don't fill your mind with other people's pain or imagined dramas - Fill your mind with healthy and positive experiences - and see the difference it makes.

If you choose to take on board only one chapter of this book. This one will bring you the greatest rewards in the shortest possible time.

Chapter 12
Good Distractions Get Things Done

In this chapter, I'm going to talk about why it's important to have distractions. That may sound odd after reading about the importance of avoiding another person's drama. So, hear me out, and I'll explain.

Distractions can be very positive things when they're managed the right way. Imagine you're working on a big project and putting in long hours - which often happens when you initially get things started. With a heightened sense of purpose, you're pushing forward with your ideas and plans to bring everything together. At times like these, it's important to have a break.

That's why it's important to have distractions.

The problem is, if you don't organize these distractions for yourself, you risk giving control to outside influences. When you give that control to outside influences, it means that you're losing a level of control in your life.

That's why it's both imperative and logical to actively take control of your distractions. Plus, there's a good reason why you'll hear me regularly mention how important it is to learn new skills and how essential it is to have hobbies. Think about it! When your project comes to fruition, the ideal is that you will have lots of spare time and the money to enjoy that spare time.

If you don't have any hobbies, chances are... you will be feeling a bit lost, not knowing what to do with your time means that you could once again allow external distractions - that you have less control over, come into play and manifest as bad habits.

Taking control of these distractions early in your development as an entrepreneur is most important.

Let's take a closer look at what good distractions really are. I understand these distractions are a healthy way for the mind to organize itself and take a break. Let's face it: we all need to take a break at some point. It doesn't matter what we're doing, even if we're doing the most pleasurable, exciting, and interesting thing. You still need to take a break because of the basic human need for variety.

This applies to all conscious time spent and experienced. Even if your everyday state of being is spent in complete luxury, there will be a point at which the mind processes it as boring or mundane.

Try this simple exercise, which may be hard to accept or digest. Think about something that you really enjoyed doing. Imagine that you have a magic lamp that will grant you the wish to enjoy the experience over and repeatedly. Hold that thought; you will continuously experience that enjoyment for the next hour, day, or even a whole week. Can you honestly say that you will not have the thought at some point I would like to take a break?

We can all get too much of a good thing. That's why variety is essential. So, how do we go about organizing our good distractions?

It's quite easy. We consciously set up our much-needed distractions in an orderly manner. Or we can prime the situation so that we have no choice but to pursue the distraction. By doing this consciously, we ensure that the distraction isn't a negative thing that will be detrimental or set us back. The distraction that's consciously set up is always going to be a positive thing because it's going to enhance our confidence and enhance our experience. It will also positively improve our skills in other areas of life. This is a key point. The distraction should not be in the area or subject that we're pursuing as our main goal.

It's done just for pure indulgence and enjoyment.

So, how can you easily do this? The best way to explain is to use an example from my list of good distractions. One of my favorite hobbies is making cheese. I love eating it, but I get the most pleasure from the process of making it.

A third element gives me a huge amount of satisfaction, too. I love sharing it with other people. If I know that we have a family event coming up in, say, three- or four months' time. I'll buy the milk and ingredients I need to make the cheese and commit to myself. Next, I'll make myself accountable by telling family or friends that I'll make cheese for our gathering.

The great thing about buying milk is it needs to be used by a certain date. I certainly don't have enough room in my freezer to store 30 milk liters (about 7.93 gal). So, I first decide when I need to buy the milk. That's my first commitment. I also make sure I set time aside in my diary to be able to make it. Depending on the type of cheese I'm making - I'll choose the evening beforehand to prepare all the utensils. Every action I take to make the cheese is part of the commitment. Each component is helping me to follow through with my intention.

The act of making cheese, compared to my full-time projects, is a distraction. It's a great distraction because I love every moment of it. As I've already said, I enjoy the process of making it, love eating it, and get a lot of pleasure from sharing it.

Can you see what's happening here, I'm setting myself up for many great experiences.

By committing myself to having a distraction from my day-to-day work, I am enhancing my life and adding to that much-needed variety. Can you think of any examples that you could apply to your life? If you can, write them down. If you can't think of any immediately, think about what you really enjoy doing, then think if there are ways that you can commit yourself to doing it in a positive way so there's no getting out of it.

Remember, you need several small commitments that hold you to task, and you also need to tell the world that you're doing it to stay accountable.

To sum up the process: Make those micro-commitments to yourself by taking the small steps needed and then set up your accountability filter by telling others what you are doing – What used to be easy to put off is now set in stone and has a massively high chance of happening – how cool is that!

If you do put off your plans, your mind's intrinsic need for variety will start to force other distractions upon you. Anyone who works online will find it very easy to get distracted. Small things such as following posts on Facebook or viewing videos. If you're into technology – you can easily find yourself watching the latest shiny object or gadget that's being promoted by marketers.

These are what I call controlling distractions. These fleeting distractions can take up a huge amount of your time. When you break it down, think about it: 5 minutes here, 5 minutes there. In a week, we're talking hours lost to these controlling distractions. Why? because your mind needed a break and some variety. In simple terms, it wanted an excuse to take a rest from plowing the same old field.

The best way to avoid these has nothing to do with abstinence and everything to do with focusing your attention on the things in life that you enjoy doing - and finding ways to set yourself up to 'have to' do them. Commit yourself 100% and put in place the things needed to make it happen, and there's no getting out of it.

In my earlier cheese-making example, I bought the right amount of milk needed. Then, I organize enough time to get everything done. For this example, we'll assume it's a Friday morning. I made a conscious decision to take a break from working. I'm going to make cheese instead.

This isn't just a simple case of putting a date and time in the diary and committing. There's a much bigger picture; let me explain… When I think about the amount of time I set aside to make cheese, I also experience, in my mind's eye, everything linked to the process. I'm imagining the pleasure of eating it and the pleasure of sharing it with family and friends. By doing this, I'm actively feeding the whole cheesemaking process with some powerful - feel-good emotions, and at the same time, I'm training my mind to associate the experience with a huge amount of pleasure.

This energy drives me forward and fills me with enthusiasm – to the point where I cannot wait until Friday to come. There's a common expression here that I mention many times throughout the book: ' Drives me forward.'

Why? Because that's where we all need to go. Forward, not standing still. Not going backward. You must always be driving forward. By now, you may be thinking that 'distractions' are a strange subject to talk about. They're not strange at all and are an essential part of your journey.

Driving forward and taking control, not being controlled, is a key element when it comes to having the strength to persevere with everything we do.

Chapter 13
The Power of Word Association

When we think about the meaning of words, what they mean to us quite often has different meanings to that of a standard dictionary. For example, when we consider the word 'discipline,' it can immediately conjure up negative associations. For many people, the word discipline may take them back to a time when they suffered discipline at the hands of a headmaster/mistress or teacher.

This was at a time in their lives when they were essentially being domesticated. It was a time when they needed discipline and taught how to toe the line and comply with the way school or society wanted them to act. This can be the same way many of us think about the word 'strict.' Again, the word conjures up images of a hard-nosed disciplinarian, strict and unwavering.

If we experience these associations during childhood, we continue to experience the word in our adult mind. Similar word associations will apply to a unique vocabulary, dating back to when we were children. During that stage in our lives, we were learning about thousands of new things every day. Then, once we become adults, everything changes. The problem is those word associations stick with us.

Because the word 'discipline' is very important for us in adult life - It's not something we should negatively associate with.

The word 'strict' is another positive word for us to embrace as adults. In the context of perseverance, it's important to have discipline. It's important to be strict with oneself. In fact, the word strict is mentioned if you look up the meaning of perseverance. It's about applying certain rules to oneself, which means exerting a high level of control.

This self-control is a positive thing. It's not someone controlling us against our will. The best thing about self-control is that it gives us exponentially more back regarding personal growth and development.

As a child, you may have been called stubborn. Now that you're an adult, that stubbornness can mature and develop into steadfastness, standing fast, and standing by what you believe. To stand by your values. This is another important transition from childhood to adulthood.

When we have a high level of self-discipline as an adult - in many cases, it's because we've experienced an external form of discipline as a child. If done with the right intention and with loving care, discipline applied to the child can work to sow the seeds that internalize in adult life. Unfortunately, if we hang onto the old experience with a negative outlook - if we hold onto those associations that that tell us that discipline is something to resist and to move away from and strictness is something to dislike, we are doing ourselves a great disservice as adults.

Every day when I started to write this book, I disciplined myself to put together at least one thousand words. I knew that those small chunks of work would eventually come together to produce a body of work. A body of work that was based on my own experiences and the knowledge I gained moving from childhood to adulthood.

No one forced me to write these words. No one said you must do this. Even though I accepted that I may never sell a single copy, I still applied a high level of strictness to commit time every day and keep to my resolve. In 30 days, I wrote 30k words.

I decided that I had to do the work to get this done. At first, writing tens of thousands of words seemed overwhelming. In college, putting together a ten-thousand-word assignment was a mammoth task. But I had to do it. Writing this book is the single biggest project I've ever done. Plus, it's a task that will put my character and abilities under scrutiny, not by a college tutor but by the people who read my book. The only way I can do this is by committing myself, being disciplined, and having strength and purpose.

My purpose is to produce this book. I am aware that I need to persevere against all odds. That's exactly what perseverance is: to keep going against all odds. The great news is you can tilt the odds in your favor by making small shifts to your attitude and beliefs.

I'll explain by giving you another example of poor word association. Think about the words that describe what you must do. Then look deep inside and ask yourself, am I associating negative things around the words that will help me propel myself forward? If you are making negative associations, where are those associations coming from?

I guarantee the associations will come from the life you used to lead, a life when you were learning the basic rules of life. The problem is, you're not learning those basic rules of life now. Hopefully, you've learned them already. Hopefully, you're fully engaging in life. You've learned those lessons; you understand the reasons behind the lessons, and you're successfully applying the skills that you've learned. You've learned self-discipline. You've learned to be strict with yourself.

Once again, I'm not suggesting that you are strict with yourself as a punishment, but as a way and a tool that will help you achieve great things in life.

The point I'm making here is, don't think with a child's mind when you're an adult. Let go of it. Let go of those thoughts, those associations. They served you perfectly well as a child. But as an adult, you need to raise the bar. You need to accept that things are different now and that you are responsible for yourself.

This is another powerful word—responsibility. OR the ability to respond appropriately. Can you respond appropriately to the work that needs to be done?

Yes, you can. You can If you've cast off the old word associations. Look for them in the way you speak, in the things you do, and in the way you look at the world, and ask yourself this question. 'Am I thinking with my child's mind or with my adult mind?'

This simple exercise will help shift your behavior and unblock many barriers to success, whatever success might mean to you.

Chapter 14
You Become What You Think About

In this section, I want to explore how we impact our own experiences, our lives, and the outcomes of our lives. I'm not speaking about the actions we take. I'm talking about the thoughts that we create. Naturally, some of you reading this will be thinking, how can thoughts impact the outcomes of my life?

Let me make a bold prediction before I explain any more. Soon, scientists will prove, without doubt, that our thoughts directly affect our reality more than our actions do.

One of the most influential books I've ever read is 'The Greatest Secret' by Earl Nightingale, not to be confused with the popular 'The Secret,' which is a much later variation about mind over matter. What Earl Nightingale wrote was summed up in 7 words, "We become what we think about mostly." Think about it, the power of thought, and how it impacts our lives. Earl was surely a genius of his time, and yet few people have heard of him.

Think about those seven words for a moment—' we become.'

That's a powerful opening statement. Then he says, 'What we think about,' the things that we think about are what we become. Then he adds the word 'mostly'

The things we think about mostly, the things that take prominence in our minds. Is what we become. That can be both a sobering and a frightening idea. If you're harboring negative thoughts, if you're constantly criticizing the world around you, and if you're constantly criticizing the world inside you. If you're feeling worthless, unworthy, or less than you really are, then that's what you become.

A negative self-fulfilling prophesy – a negative feedback loop.

On the other hand, if you're expanding your mind and your perceptions, you're generating positive thoughts and realizing that you have amazing potential as a human being, and you can and will overcome all obstacles. That will become true, too. This takes us back to perseverance. When we move forward and push against all obstacles, against all barriers, no matter what, we achieve success.

Can you see the direct link between positive thought and perseverance? If our positive attitude and thoughts move us forward and help us to overcome barriers, we are working with perseverance. We're going in the right direction with our thoughts, and our actions naturally follow.

I'm not going to put a percentage on how much I think our thoughts impact our lives. Whatever it may be, whatever scientists, psychologists, or psychiatrists have to say in years to come, I feel certain that it will be far greater than anyone imagined.

It's reasonable to argue that if we become what we think about mostly, thoughts affect our actions before the action happens. If every action must have a thought to bring it to life. Consider just how powerful and how potent that is.

What are you creating with your thoughts? Are you creating a positive and powerful environment and driving you forward, or are you going in the opposite direction? Are you sabotaging your efforts?

Sabotaging our efforts isn't always a conscious thing. As I've said before, you may have some bad habits in your psychology. You're thinking with your child's mind, a mind that served you perfectly well throughout childhood. You're still thinking with that mindset. Whatever it is that you're doing, you need to take a high level of control over your thought processes. What comes to mind when you ask yourself the question, "What message am I sending out into my world with my thoughts, what am I co-creating with the universe?"

When I say universe, I don't want this to come across as being a spiritual work. I don't see myself as being in any way qualified to do that. When I use the word universe, I just mean the world around you. Your environment, the people around you, your sphere of influence.

We become what we think about mostly. Just take a few moments to consider that statement again. And I'd highly recommend reading or listening to The Greatest Secret by Earl Nightingale. I think the last time I watched it was on YouTube. It also comes in the form of audio recordings. It's a powerful message. It's a message written decades ago, yet it still applies and always will because I believe it to be a universal truth.

In fact, that statement is one of the most powerful statements to impact my life. I read it when I was in my 30s. I've always been interested in reading about psychology, the mind over matter, and the subtler things in life. I have hundreds of books, and every day, I get some new information. This information is usually related to how we navigate the world, how our minds work, how we fit in with everything, and how this impacts our lives and other people's lives. I see it as a social responsibility to provide myself with the best information possible.

By adopting this habit, I get a great amount of pleasure. One of the greatest pleasures I get is sharing some of that information, whether it be with friends, colleagues, or my children. Or a stranger. It gives me a great amount of pleasure to offer up an idea, a new perspective, not in a preachy way but in a practical and valuable way. Make this your practice if you enjoy reading and taking in new information. Get into the habit of bookmarking the things that stand out for you. The things that you find useful, there's going to be a good chance that other people will find that useful too, and by sharing that information, you're putting out some powerful and positive vibes into the world.

By doing this, people will value you as being a source of positive knowledge and information. This also puts you in a good light… and trust me, it will bring opportunities beyond your imagination. People will trust you when you share some information that works out for someone. When someone has a light bulb moment, an a-ha moment, or says, "That's perfect for me at this moment in time. I really needed to hear that." You immediately elevate your positioning, you increase your 'average rating' within their minds.

Read more, learn about the workings of the mind, about human beings, and how we operate. Read a wide variety of books on the subject. Don't get stuck in one groove or become an evangelist about one subject. Variety is key.

If you don't like reading books, or for some reason you cannot read books, there are plenty of opportunities to listen to books on audio. One of the great resources I use is Audible. Audible has thousands and thousands of books in its library, and for a small subscription, every month, I choose one new book.

Another great source of free audio and books is www.archive.org. You will find thousands of out-of-print books here and audio to download.

This type of information is positive and gets us thinking about the important things in life; it opens our minds to new ideas and expands our minds. Are you an expansive person? Or do you restrict your thoughts? Do you keep your mind broad? Or are you narrow-minded? Consider these questions because they will help you push forward. They will help you on your journey to strengthen your thinking and your ability to master your life.

Chapter 15
You Need to Avoid Critical Exposure Overload

I want to share something closely related to this book's overall theme, and that is the thoughts we keep. There are two areas in life where our thoughts influence our mindset. One of them greatly disables us, and the other one helps us. I'll talk about the one that disables us first. We live in a world that is very critical. The newspapers criticize celebrities; we criticize each other, our friends, and our neighbors. These might not be outright criticisms, but they're still judgments, and the ego story that we tell ourselves often goes something like, "They're doing this, and they're doing it wrong, and I know better." Sounds familiar?

It's this kind of critical attitude that damages our mental health. Why does it damage our mental health? I believe it damages it because it harbors negativity, which is not a healthy path to pursue. When we criticize others, we put them down. In some respects, you could say we put others down to lift ourselves up.

But why would we need to do that? Do we have such a poor image of ourselves that we must put others down to lift ourselves up?

Maybe we do. Maybe we do have poor images of ourselves. Maybe we do have little self-esteem. But honestly, does that justify spending an inordinate amount of time having critical thoughts or judging other people by standards we can't even keep ourselves?

If you think about the anatomy of thought forms, we tell ourselves a story, and the story that we tell ourselves has a beginning, a middle, and an end. That's how stories work.

And the story that we tell ourselves when we're criticizing others is simply, they're wrong, and I'm right, and that makes me happy. That is a very sad story. To judge others for such superficial things as their clothes, their cars, their jobs, their income, maybe how they look—things that they can't possibly change, that they haven't got control over. Maybe we criticize somebody for their parenting skills, or we criticize somebody for what they say. It's all about you wanting to be right and making them wrong.

Humans want to be right all the time, and humility seems to be in short supply. Imagine if you can foster a mindset that enjoys not being right always. A mindset that enjoys getting it wrong, and when you do get it wrong, you say to yourself, "I recognize that I was wrong, and I know that I can learn from that." Getting it wrong then becomes a gift, an opportunity to learn. The problem occurs when you get it wrong repeatedly because that's not progressing. That's simply being stuck, and being stuck isn't healthy either.

Making judgments and assumptions about how things are in someone else's life is superficial. You may view someone's life from the outside - just a small vignette of their life and yet jump to conclusions. Unfortunately, conclusions are illusions—they're not real. Everyone has their path, and their journey; they don't need your judgments. Psychologically, that's a form of trespass.

You might see somebody sitting in the street; why make the judgment they're a loser, and they need to try harder? You don't know their story; you don't know where they are at that moment, and you don't know what strength they've got to pull themselves up and get themselves out of that situation. Maybe sitting begging on the street is exactly where they need to be at this moment. The universe isn't stupid, and it isn't random. Are you going to argue with the universe, good luck with that.

Everyone has a story. I once read that every beggar has a future, and every prince has a past. And it's true. We judge so quickly, and we're so critical of people's circumstances and their choices. By doing this, we rob ourselves of something vital because we take on board negativity that eats away at the very source of energy that we need to achieve things for ourselves. By judging others, we are holding ourselves back.

Be aware of the criticisms and judgments you make daily; simply watch out for them. When you watch out for them, you hold them in conscious awareness. If you hold them in conscious awareness, you can do something about it. You can change the thoughts that you harbor.

Simply say to yourself, "I'm aware I'm being quite critical, and I don't like the way that makes me feel." Looking at how it makes you feel, you realize it's not a good feeling. It doesn't lift you up, it doesn't boost your energy, it doesn't enliven you. It takes something away. It wastes your vital energy, you may call that mental energy, you may call that negativity. You can call it what you like. But it's a fact when we criticize others, when we make judgments when we gossip about people, which is another way that we make criticism, by gossiping about people, by making judgments, by making ourselves right and them wrong. It's all an ego-centered thing, and it's a very common thing to do. But it's not healthy.

On the flip side, you can increase your energy and positivity by showing respect. There's an old word that's not used very often these days. Veneration, by holding someone in veneration, to hold them up as being great contributors, as being incredible and positive people.

It may be that you love music or sport, or maybe you admire someone who is an industrialist or an entrepreneur, an anthropologist—whoever it is, those great writers out there in literature, some of them have achieved such amazing things, contributed so much to humanity. These people earn your respect. A respect for what they have achieved and what they have contributed. Some of them you will venerate.

From a very young age, I read a lot. One writer stood out for me, I instantly resonated with his philosophy and teachings. This was the Austrian philosopher and teacher Rudolph Steiner. Rudolph Steiner was most prolific with his writings, not only in his writings but also in life. He would lecture tirelessly day after day after day. He was born in Austria; his father was a railway signalman, so he didn't come from a wealthy family. But he got where he got through his hard work, his dedication, and his vision.

Steiner wrote hundreds of books. He contributed to medicine. He contributed to agriculture. He contributed to art. He contributed to a huge number of areas that are still being followed today. His teachings and his ideas are still being acted upon today. Thousands and thousands of people around the world work in businesses and educational establishments. All stemming from one man's work, Rudolph Steiner.

I had the pleasure of visiting his university in Switzerland when I was in my mid-20s. I bought a cheap rail ticket to travel around Europe, and I thought what a great opportunity it would be to see the university there in front of me, in real life, to witness someone's achievement in the form of a grandiose building like no other. I was lucky to stay in a small guest house near the university. I remember opening the curtains in the morning and seeing the university building and its incredible structure. I was absolutely blown away. I was in awe, I was inspired. If you are curious about what I saw, search images for Goetheanum.

That one person could achieve so much in a lifetime gave me a huge amount of motivation. I'm not saying I would end up being an educationalist, teacher, architect, or any of those things. I was simply going to contribute my small part to the world. It gave me the impetus, it gave me that feeling, that sense of veneration towards someone who'd achieved so much.

And in many cases, against all odds, Steiner achieved so much. Of course there are many writers, there are many teachers, there are many people throughout history who have achieved so much. Consider this to immerse yourself in some of the work they've done. Look at their lives, read their biographies - whatever you can do, expose yourself to the details and information available about them. Because in a powerful way, it will pick you up, inspire you, and propel you mentally. It gives you something so positive it pushes you forward; it shows you that there is a way because others before you have achieved so much.

Whatever you want to achieve, you can achieve. Other people have achieved what they wanted to achieve, and so can you. You must take those first steps. For me, one of those steps was to reduce the amount of critical thinking and judgment I made of others. No one likes to be judged. I know, for one, from a very young age, I hated to be criticized. It used to really get my backup. It would make me feel quite angry. I understand that now, I understand where that came from.

I figured if I didn't like being criticized directly, why would I want to do it to other people? Harboring these critical thoughts drains our energy. So, instead of harboring critical thoughts, spend more time looking at what great people have done, what they've achieved, and what they've contributed. We live in the age of communication. It's easy to find out anything you want. It doesn't cost the earth to search for information or to download an eBook.

Years ago, you'd have had to go to a library; years ago, you'd have had to buy a book. You don't have to buy the book. It's never been easier to get the information. Find at least one person that you can read about, you can find out about, you can study. Feel a difference in your life. And at the same time, be aware of criticism in your life. Be aware of the judgments you make, and you'll see a massive shift and an increase in the energy you have each day to put into your projects.

Instead of depleting your energy, you'll boost your energy, and that's an important resource for anybody who wants to achieve anything.

CHAPTER 16
OUR BIG PROBLEM WITH JUDGMENTS

Regarding making judgments - not about other people, but judgments about things that happen, there's always a tendency to want to put that experience into a box quickly. To label it. Human beings love to label things. It's almost as if we need to label it, and then we put it on the shelf. And that's it. We're done with it. And we can go about doing other things.

The problem with this is we tend to have default labels. Labels are very definite and defined. An example might be that you miss the bus. You didn't have an appointment, but you still missed the bus and judged that as bad. It's so bad; I've missed the bus, experienced, labeled, and shelved. But then, while standing at the bus stop waiting for the next bus, someone that you recognize arrives. You haven't seen them for years. You get into a conversation, and you thoroughly enjoy the experience. It was nice to see them and hear about what's been happening in their life, and you could just as easily say, that's good, I'm glad I missed the bus.

Can you see when we quickly give experiences labels? That's bad, I missed the bus. It never ever goes right for me, etc... The poor me story continues. And so, we set ourselves on this negative train of thought. Imagine if you set yourself on that negative train of thought - I missed the bus, nothing ever goes right for me, and you start to get yourself into this mental turmoil; chances are, you wouldn't have seen the person walking up to the bus stop. You wouldn't have recognized them because you're too busy looking inward.

Some people may express an experience as feeling good. And then I found out it wasn't so good after all. What I'm suggesting is to exercise some curiosity. Reserve judgment, be curious, and be interested in what experiences really mean. A good way of doing this is to look at an experience afterward, but not look at it as though you're yourself; look at it as if witnessing as a third party. Consider it. Consider what happened. Be curious, be interested. This can be a great way of exercising self-reflection.

When we judge something as good or bad, we rob ourselves of that experience. Now, some people may be reading this who think, yeah, well, what if something bad happens? Someone gets killed, someone gets murdered. I agree; there are certain circumstances in which it would be very difficult not to judge as bad. What I'm saying here is not to look for the extremes to prove your argument but look at the day-to-day experiences in between, where it clearly isn't that bad. But still, we are quick to judge it as being bad. Exercise some curiosity.

Get out of the habit of labeling everything instantly because experiences don't happen in a vacuum. One experience leads to another experience, a chain of events. There's never nothing going on. Life is an interconnected series of experiences. And that's important to recognize. It's important to accept that fact.

Another useful exercise is to write out your timeline.

A simple timeline of your life, and on that timeline, add some major experiences. Some real juicy things happened, which, at the time, you might have judged as being bad. Write out that timeline starting from your earliest memories and then add significant points along the way. Add those experiences that, at the time, you would have judged as being bad.

When you've done that, sit back and consider the things that have happened since those experiences directly related to what happened. It may have been that your father had a business, and you had to close because of bad debt. And because of that, you had to move house. For many people, that will be seen as a bad experience, traumatic, and humiliating.

But then, look at the other things that have happened because of that. Because of that experience, the opportunities that have risen, the things that have opened for you, and how that has changed your life. So, on reflection, had that thing not happened, that thing you labeled as bad at the time, had that not happened, those other series of events wouldn't have happened either.

Those series of events which you know have enriched your life and maybe, well, depending on how old you are, maybe you wouldn't have met the love of your life had you not been in that new place due to the circumstances that had happened before. You may not have been given the opportunity to work at that company, to study at that university or college, to meet friends, and ultimately have the family that you have had those 'bad' experiences not happen in the first place.

So, in some way, you could say, in hindsight, it was good that your father lost his business because of bad debt. It meant that you moved to a different area, and that just happened to be near the university where you studied. You wouldn't have studied there otherwise, and you met that person, those people at university, you become lifelong friends with, and one of them, you married. And you've got children, and you look at your children now, and you can see that there are so many things that you could have judged as bad within that timeline. But actually, were blessings in disguise.

So, exercise withholding judgment about your experience. Create a new label. Call it the 'I'm curious' label. And see what happens. See what unfolds. Not everything that we label as good or bad in the immediate moment is really so. And by accepting that, you open more opportunities, it opens up your mind, and you might be thinking, how does that help me with regards to having perseverance?

Well, anything that helps you get a perspective on life. Anything that doesn't hold you back or gives you an element of positivity massively impacts the amount of energy and attention you can give to your projects.

Why, because you become CLEAR.

If you said, "Oh, this is so bad, and that's so bad, as you can imagine, " that isn't the greatest mindset for someone trying to persevere. This habit of labeling will eventually attach those labels to the project you're working on. It's going to get infected. And it's important not to infect the things you're trying to achieve with your immediate judgments about circumstances that might not be so. So, withhold judgment. And be curious. Create a new label.

Chapter 17
Making Your Master Plan

In this chapter, I want to talk about making plans. When it comes to perseverance, it's very important to get into the mindset of making plans. I don't want to talk about small-scale plans. Not small project plans. Everyone has their own style in the way they plan small things. Whenever he made anything out of wood, my late father would jot down a few sketches, just a few dimensions. Very basic. And yet, the final thing that he crafted was phenomenal. He made small rowing boats, elaborate cabinets, you name it, he made it all out of wood.

The only plans he ever made were scribbles in his notepad. Other people's style might have been to have technical working drawings. Everyone has a different way of planning things. It's important to do it your way. So, I'm not going to advise how to set up your goals and make your plans that way. What I want to talk about today is having a master plan.

If you imagine small plans as being detailed and, in many respects, rigid, a master plan is quite the opposite. But it's still a plan. A master plan is flexible. You see, when you start out on your journey or a project, there's no knowing how it will turn out. That's part of the excitement. Being curious about how something might work out is important.

Having a master plan is all about being flexible; unlike a blueprint, a master plan is grey. Why? because things change, as you'll see. So, a master plan is quite loose. But it is still a plan. A master plan could tell yourself, when I've achieved this, my life will be like this. In a year, I hope to work from home, working for myself. That's quite loose, working from home. You're not saying what you're doing working from home. You're not saying where your home is. Or you might add that detail. I want to work from home in my new house in the countryside.

You've added a little bit more detail. But the details are quite loose: countryside, a new house in the countryside in a year's time. Flexibility is so important because if we don't have flexibility in our master plan, there's a chance that we give up every time things don't fall into place. But when you've got flexibility in your master plan, then you allow for change. You'll find that allowing for change and having that flexibility is one of the greatest benefits and attributes of someone who cultivates perseverance in life.

Now, you might think that I ramble on about perseverance being a thing. An attitude, a discipline, but it's much more than that. Perseverance includes all these things and so much more. It's an energy. It's a force, and it's important to feed that energy and force, and it's important not to set it up to fail, and that's why it's so important to have a master plan that has a huge degree of flexibility.

In my master plan many years ago, I decided to work from home,

NEVER GIVE UP

and my working week would be split into thirds. I don't know why I came up with the idea of splitting into thirds, but it seemed like a good number. I liked the number three; good enough reason, I guessed. It wasn't complicated, which is another good reason. I decided that during my working week, I would spend a third of it working to pay the bills and maintain my lifestyle. Another third of the time I would spend prospecting.

What I mean by prospecting is doing work that isn't bringing in an immediate income. I will be doing work that may come to fruition in the future. No guarantees. It meant I would work on my own projects. This book is part of my prospecting and of course, this book is part of my master plan. I mean, why wouldn't it be?

The other third of the week, I decided I would spend learning. In any industry, it is crucial to keep learning. Within my industry, internet marketing, it's important to keep up to date with what's happening. Technology moves so fast; people's behaviors change very quickly. We need to adapt. My customers want me to keep up to date. So, I endeavor to spend a third of my week learning new skills. It might be reading. It might be listening to an audiobook or studying a new course.

It may be a new program that will make my life simpler and my time more efficient. Whatever it is, it's learning new skills. So that's my master plan. It's very loose and some weeks, I spend more time learning than I do prospecting. Other weeks I spend more time working than I do learning. There's a healthy degree of flexibility. I don't beat myself up because I spent all week working because I've got a big project for a client.

That's okay. The week after, I might spend all week learning. Flexibility is so important. No one is standing over me; that's the great thing about working for oneself. There's no one standing over me telling me I've got to do this; I've got to do that. I have deadlines for clients, and I try to make sure these are realistic and achievable. That's just planning on a small scale. But planning on the big scale, the master plan, you can furnish that with anything you want.

Some people like to make vision boards. Big sheets of cards with pictures of the things they want and to achieve stuck on. The only thing is, when they stick the pictures down, it kind of makes it a little bit rigid. So, that wouldn't be my way of doing it. I'm a very visual person, and I can imagine things, so I see things in my mind's eye, a bit like my father; if I'm making something out of wood, I draw a very minimal number of details, and I build it in my head. That's how I work. It's different for everyone. Having that degree of flexibility is essential but most important of all, having a plan, a master plan, a big plan for your life is essential to move forward because you know where you're moving towards. It's not a straight line. It will never be a straight line. Life doesn't work in straight lines.

Having that degree of curiosity means that your expectations aren't damaged when something doesn't work out. As I've mentioned before in this book, sometimes an action and the outcome aren't what you expected. Though often, it leads you onto things that work out even better than expected or a different direction altogether. Good fortune isn't always instantly recognized. It's like a good wine or a good cheese. It can take time to develop and mature and depends greatly on its environment and the conditions in which you keep it.

Having a master plan is like having the right conditions. It's like having an umbrella over all your ideas, but the umbrella can get wider or tighten closer, depending on the circumstances at the time. Don't necessarily write this down now, but have an idea of what your master plan looks like. Where will you be living? Maybe not specifically, but maybe near the coast. What will you be doing? Not specifically, but loosely, what will you be doing?

Will you be helping people? That's a loose plan to be helping people because there are lots of ways to help people. Being creative that's a loose definition because there are lots of ways of being creative. Try not to narrow it right down to the specific details. Allow that degree of flexibility. And hold that in your mind's eye, and as things or circumstances change, it's okay to change your master plan. No one is going to measure it. Not even you. Because there's no need. Because it is fluid. That's the whole point of all of this. Is to have a degree of fluidity.

If you're a perfectionist, you may find this exercise difficult because you want things to be just so, but when do things ever really happen just so? Do we think we're Gods and can control everything around us? Then we're fooling ourselves. There may be a subtle interplay going on in our lives; I don't doubt that. That's what makes me curious. It can also help you find your purpose and your passion. Having a master plan will link you and connect you with your purpose. I can see this evolving in my life. I'm curious what the next step might be. I'm curious how this book might be received. That excites me. I don't see it as being an opportunity for failure or success. For me, the achievement is finishing the book and seeing it in print. I can take care of all of that because of all the small plans I've made. They've all brought me to this place. All the new learning and experiences, all the projects I've worked on for clients, and the prospecting that I've done have brought me to where I am today, and I'm full of gratitude for those experiences.

The important thing is, if I'd been rigid with my plans, then I may have stumbled at the first hurdle. Build your master plan. Keep it loose. Allow it to change. Hold it in your mind's eye and heart and be curious about how it evolves. And I guarantee you'll get there a lot quicker than you could ever imagine.

Chapter 18
Myth Busting Your Superstitions

In this chapter, I will talk about superstitions and myths and how they can help and hinder our perseverance. Every culture, society, and age has its myths. And its superstitions. And if you take a superstition and look back at its origins, you'll see that it's quite often based on facts. Things that have been passed down, certain behaviors, culturally over time. Superstitions are born out of behavior and experience. It is worth exploring some of these within your own life and culture, just to their origins.

It will open your mind and give you an idea of how powerful superstition is. Superstitions are also time-based within our history, and what may have served people well back then, culturally, hinders society today. Set yourself some time aside and explore. I won't give examples here of cultural superstitions; we all have our own. Explore them, and think of ones from your childhood.

There are huge resources on the internet to research these types of things. Don't spend too much time exploring; simply familiarize yourself with one or two out of curiosity.

Beyond cultural superstitions, there are personal superstitions. We all have personal superstitions. One of my superstitions that stands out for me is that I should never tell anyone about a project I am working on because it would Jinx it; it would somehow bring me bad luck. When I look at this personal superstition and dive in and explore it deeper, I can see where it comes from. I can see it comes from a fear of failure. If I'm going to do something special and I tell someone I'm going to do it, and then they ask me how it is going, and it didn't work out. That feels like I'm admitting defeat; it's admitting failure.

It feels embarrassing, so exploring my personal myth as an adult made me realize that I could re-engineer it slightly. I would tell people once I'd started a project. So instead of saying to people, friends, and relatives, I'm going to do something, which was essentially a promise of words, I would say, I've started a project and share some details. When I started writing this book, I remembered telling my son, and he'd ask what it is about. How big is it going to be? And would it be a physical book?

The amount of information I already had I could share with him. Naturally, he was interested and commented, "Oh, that sounds great; it sounds like a great project and a great subject." I remember telling my brother he's a teacher, and I told him I was writing a book. He asked what it was about. I told him I'd already done 10,000 words. He asked how long it would be, and I explained that it would be around 40,000 words.

Those are real, tangible, solid details. They're not, I'm thinking of doing, or I'm going to do this or that. Those tangible things

I shared are how I shifted my superstition, I gave it some real meat, I gave it some real detail. I proved my intention to write a book by giving solid details.

After changing my superstition, I later learned that telling people what you're doing massively increases your chances of success. I did some research on this; loosely, it claimed that if you decide that you're going to do something, you've probably got a 20 percent chance of success. That's not bad: one in five chances of success. The same study showed that if you decide to do something you promise yourself to follow through with it, and make a detailed plan, you increase your chances of success to around 50 percent. At the time, I thought, yeah, that makes sense; not many things work without some kind of plan, whether it's a scrap of paper or detailed working drawing or full schematic of what you'll do with timelines depending on your style. That's going to increase it by 50 percent. That's a huge increase.

What really shocked me, the thing that blows my original superstition out the water, is when you tell someone else what you're doing and your plans, you increase your success to 85 percent. Now, that's a massive shift.

In a nutshell, if you decide you're going to do something. Then, you start the project and establish some tangible details to share with others. Then you tell someone about it, you increase your chances of success four-fold.

Can you see the paradox here? My superstition, and I know many people share it, had me believe that if I tell someone what I'm doing, I risk looking stupid. When in truth, if I tell someone what I'm planning/doing, I increase my chances of succeeding by 400%.

Look how incredibly different that is because of a limiting belief.

Another wonderful cultural myth I've often heard is the claim that people can become overnight successes.

Then I read a sobering antidote to this myth: someone said, "It took me 30 years to become an overnight success." That brought everything into perspective because, let's face it, people love to read about miracles and urban myths. They don't talk about the years of struggle, pain, and failed attempts. Then I read someone else make a similar statement, "I've been a very successful failure for 40 years." Which resonated with me, having lost several businesses in my lifetime.

As you've probably guessed, I regret none of it. I regret none of it because it brought me to where I am today, and I wouldn't change anything.

So, look at your own personal myths, your own personal beliefs, and your own personal superstitions, and challenge them. Do a bit of research and see if there's been a bit of social psychology around that superstition. Explore some of the myths from your own culture, from your own childhood, from your own background. Look at those myths and see how they can be challenged and if the opposite is true.

Those myths that you hold onto may be holding you back. It's all about questioning your perspective. Something that we accept as a given is usually dysfunctional and old ways of thinking.

I've talked in this book about thinking with a child's mind, a child's experience, and how it's served us perfectly well as a child, because we didn't know better. We didn't have many tools to work with. But now that we do, it's about shifting from the old way of thinking into a new mode of thinking. By being more critical and a bit more scientific with our thinking, we discover that science has already debunked the myth of "If I tell someone my plans, I will increase my chances of failure."

A stupid myth that was based on my fear of looking stupid could not have been more wrong. I find it refreshing to discover that I got something so wrong. I find it refreshing because I know that I've grown. In a small way, I've expanded. I've become more complete.

Challenge your myths, challenge your superstitions. Explore them. It's great fun. I highly recommend it. It may be that one simple silly myth is holding you back.

Imagine putting 100 percent effort and energy into something and finding out that you're sabotaging the results by maybe 80 percent. All because you're holding onto a belief that is simply not true, and it turns out that the reality is it works positively in your favor. Now, that's insanity, as far as I'm concerned. That's pure craziness. But it is still refreshing to discover.

So, try to undo some of that craziness. It's easy to do. You just have to be willing to explore and apply a little bit of self-reflection and some self-inquiry. Ask yourself, "What am I doing right now that I'm simply accepting as a given when really the opposite could be as true?" It is great exercise, and I highly recommend it.

Chapter 19
Learning to Celebrate Your Achievements

In this chapter, we will look at the power of celebrating achievements. I find it strange that we human beings don't spend much time celebrating our personal achievements. Whereas we tend to enjoy celebrating other people's achievements more. It is almost as though giving yourself a pat on the back is a bit distasteful.

Personally, I think there's nothing wrong with this, and it's a great thing to do.

But imagine this: if you were writing a book, for instance. You get to the first five or ten thousand words. You see it as a milestone. You've achieved your first objective. You've achieved the first barrier to getting started. Give yourself a pat on the back, and treat yourself. When I say treat yourself, it's all down to perspective, some people might see a treat for themselves as having a slice of cake in their favorite café and enjoying a coffee on their own to celebrate that moment quietly. Whatever the treat or celebration, you give it meaning.

Humans are meaning-making machines; we give life its meaning. Can you grasp the concept that we give life its meaning? If we don't, then everyone else tells us how things should be. The media, other people, or our upbringing. We owe it to ourselves to give life its meaning. So, celebrate those milestones, those achievements, those small conquests, and be attached to those good feelings about rewarding yourself, about giving yourself a pat on the back. Not just a verbal pat on the back. Do something to anchor it to something positive and memorable. Show yourself that you've really enjoyed the experience.

Reflect on how you've overcome your own obstacles by getting started. Maybe you've given up some things that you enjoyed doing, or maybe this is more important than going out with friends. Remind yourself that you've committed to something and achieved it, and that's no small thing. See it as being significant and give it significance.

Some people might write 100,000 words and say it was no big deal.

But it was a big deal, and, in a sense, they're not acknowledging themselves. Some of us can take that kind of congratulation from external sources, but internally, it's important to do that too. Learn how to give yourself self-congratulations. It's not egotistical, it's not selfish. People call the strangest thing selfish. Giving yourself a reward isn't selfish. It's important, it's valuable, you're giving meaning to your experience and achievements.

The great part about this is it links directly to your perseverance.

You're setting up a can-do mindset, you're setting yourself up for an experience that will repeat itself repeatedly. Maybe you wrote the first five thousand words, and then after 10,000 words, you give yourself a different reward. It could be a small gesture, a bar of chocolate at the first 5,000 words. At the next milestone, you may decide to take your partner or friend out for dinner and let them know you are celebrating something important. And what they ask, "What's the occasion?" You told them, "I'm celebrating a small achievement, I've written the first 10,000 words in my new book." Let them share in your joy. Let them see that you're really enjoying it. This will set up a lot of positive energy around the experience. Then, when they ask weeks later, "Hey, how is that book going on?" You can talk about it with them and feel very positive and proud.

It is okay to receive validation from the outside, but we must also learn to receive it from ourselves. There is something strange about society today. Maybe it's the over-domestication of human beings because we view self-reward as self-centered. It's as though the word 'self' comes with some negative connotations. But in truth, at the end of the day, we only have the self; using it in this positive way helps us push forward. It recognizes the universal value of the individual.

I confess I've never been a big fan of committees. I've been invited to join some in my lifetime involving business and such. I remember reading a quote. I'm not sure who wrote it, but it went something like this: "Search the parks in all the cities, you'll find no statues of committees." That's so true. It does not take a group of people to make a difference, Individuals do things themselves greatly. We can all do great things. You are an individual. No more and no less than other individuals on this planet. Your potential and your achievements are determined by the vision that you hold in your mind. Some people come from difficult backgrounds but have achieved phenomenal things in their lives; sometimes, they do it for pure love. They did it because they were passionate about it; they did it because they had the drive and felt it was their purpose.

What's not to celebrate about that? It's something that should be celebrated. The other thing I'd like to add at the end of this section is - when people help you along the way, accept their help. And when you feel that someone has helped you in a way that was over and above what was expected, let them know that you appreciate them. Acknowledge it, and in some way, maybe offer them a reward, some value to them, to let them know that you appreciate the effort and support they gave you. That might be something simple, a thank you card maybe. There is no need for big gestures; appreciation is value.

If someone is doing a job for you, you might give them a small tip, and it says to them, that's a sign of my appreciation - I really appreciate what you've done for me. Have a beer or go and have coffee and cake on me. What you do when you do this, as well as being such a great thing to do, is help establish a connection with that person, and you link your success with their efforts. You're acknowledging the part that they have played in your success.

Okay, you may have paid them to do some work for you. But that's just a transaction; that's a business transaction. It may be that they didn't charge you, and they did it for the joy of being able to help, and that's great, too. A gesture of being able to say thank you is a great gift for all involved. Take opportunities to say thank you, not only to yourself but to other people along the way. It's important to establish this positive mindset around the things you do. Giving makes you feel just as good, if not better, than the person that you give to. How powerful is that? It's like the power of hugging someone.

Not only does it feed into your feelings of goodness, but it also makes somebody else feel great too. It doesn't cost anything to say thank you.

If you need lots of small self-worth validations, do it. It doesn't take that much time. When you think of how much time you waste on things that are less important, you will find the time, and you will see the value in it.

CHAPTER 20
TALKING AS THERAPY

There is great power in the act of talking things through. I learned the real power of talking as therapy when I was quite young. I was a teenager, and my mum suffered from bouts of depression. I found that simply sitting and listening to her and allowing her to talk through how she was feeling helped her work through the difficulties she was experiencing just by having somebody to listen. And she used to say how much I helped her. I used to think I didn't do anything; I just listened. Sometimes, I'd offer up some ideas or suggestions about how maybe the way she looked at it was inaccurate.

But I did understand, especially after hearing the stories that she had been through some really traumatic times, as a child during the war, and suffering at the hands of a wicked stepmother. So much so, she had to move out of her family home and go live with her stepsister. I understood how powerful talking could be as a therapeutic agent for change, to help shift us from one place to another.

Later in life, I studied to be a counselor. I delivered hundreds of hours of counseling volunteer work in a local center during that time. That was part of the course requirements. Also, part of the course requirements was to take part in my own counseling with a registered counselor. Both experiences reinforced my understanding and appreciation of how important and powerful it is to talk.

These clients would come with all kinds of issues, from suicidal thoughts to feelings of low self-worth to depression. One thing I found quite consistent with all these people was that they didn't have anyone to talk to. Most of these people were isolated.

I came to realize that many of these people had isolated themselves. It was like a self-fulfilling prophecy. They would often complain that they had no one in their life. And yet, they didn't do anything; they took no action and made no effort to try to communicate with other people.

They were getting exactly what they were putting out there, and they couldn't see it. It was as though their perspective had been shifted so that they couldn't see the wood for the trees.

Not having anyone to talk to severely impacted their wellbeing. Often, I would sit with them quietly and listen. And at times, I would challenge them. I would challenge the things they said in an immediate way. I would ask them, "Is that 100% true?" If they would say something like, "No one loves me," I would ask the question, "Do you know that to be 100% true, that no one on this planet loves you?

It would be interesting to see the kinds of answers that I got back, which would lead us to explore. One of my tutors said,

"There is never nothing going on." Sometimes, we would sit there in silence for half the session. I accepted it was their time, their space. I had to be there; it was part of the course. I needed to complete so many counseling hours. Clients often say, "I'm really sorry for wasting your time."

I would explain, "You're not wasting my time. I'm here even if you're not here. In fact, the fact that you're here is helping me." In some way, I believe that gave them a kind of consolation. It gave them a small significance, a sense of purpose.

So, how does this relate to the subject of perseverance? Often, when you're pushing forward, and you're trying to achieve things, and you're getting outside of your comfort zone, and you're pushing your personal boundaries, you will come up against obstacles and problems, and it's important to have a support network of people who you can talk to.

Naturally, there are some people you wouldn't talk to about certain things, and I totally understand that; I totally agree.

What's important is that you have people you can talk to and discuss the issues. There's a lot of truth in the saying that a problem shared is a problem halved. We get a lot from talking through the issues, obstacles, and problems we face. I can't over-emphasize how powerful it is to open your mouth and express your feelings.

There's something very magical going on when we open our mouths, and we speak, especially when we speak from a place that acknowledges we're not perfect. And I think it's that humility, not accepting that we're perfect, and owning that vulnerability that makes us stronger.

Now, that might seem ironic, and a lot of things in life are quite ironic. But by showing vulnerability, having the courage to express your feelings strengthens you in ways you would never imagine. It might be that you can't afford to pay to talk to someone professional. You don't always have to pay people to talk to them. Sometimes striking up a conversation with a neighbor while out walking or in the local café with one of the people serving is all it takes; try it, strike up a conversation, and ask them, how was your day?

Many people are frightened that they're not interesting, which means they're frightened of coming across as boring. That's a genuine fear in the world these days. I don't want to come across as boring because if I come across as boring, I'm a bore, and I'll be labeled a bore. Well, let me tell you. That's dysfunctional thinking. Because you don't have to be interesting to be of interest to other people. You see, the secret to being interesting is by being interested in other people.

When you start a conversation and ask someone how they are, you give something of yourself. There's an interplay, there's a dynamic that's going on that is so rich and connects you at such a subtle level, that person sees you as being an interesting person because you are interested in them. Can you see how this works? By showing interest in other people, by talking to people. Engaging and entering their world can give you something so rich and so valuable in return.

Now you might think, well, I didn't do anything, and in a sense, you didn't have to do anything apart from show interest, and the person will open. It's like having a magic key. The person opens up to you and says and starts to tell you things. Have you ever had it where you'll be talking to someone, and they'll say I can't believe I just told you all of that about my life. I never told anyone about that before. That's a very common thing to happen.

And it doesn't happen because you're a fabulous therapist or have some magical skills. It happens because you showed interest and you opened that person up.

Think of the expressions that we use in life. People say, I just clam up. I can't make myself vulnerable by sharing. By sharing, you make yourself open to possibilities. And when you're trying to achieve great things, when you're trying to overcome obstacles, when you're trying to push through and persevere, there's one thing I will guarantee you - you will come up against things that will require help from other people.

And that help may simply be in the form of someone hearing you. Being heard, being a voice amongst millions, can feel very empowering in that it gives you the power to overcome the obstacle in front of you. You don't need any special skills; you don't need any special knowledge. But the fact that you're feeling heard helps you dig right down deep into yourself and find the strength and the energy that was always there. You see, I believe that our problems are given to us as gifts.

I know some people might disagree and say, "How can you say that? There might be some extreme problems; how can you see that as a gift?" I'm not judging that; it's just my belief. A belief that everything that meets us in life meets us for a reason. As I've said before, judging whether it's good or bad is not useful. Being curious about what it brings, how it contributes to life, and the opportunities it opens is useful. And we can't know that in advance.

All obstacles are opportunities. I'm not being flippant when I say that. They are opportunities, they're opportunities to grow.

There is no growth in content. There's no progress in feeling contented. Of course, we can all feel pleased with where we are. I feel very happy with my lot. My life. My circumstances. I feel very happy. But I don't sit back and say that's it, I've made it now, I don't have to worry about anything else. I enjoy challenges. I enjoy growing. I enjoy feeling the pains, the growing pains of learning something new.

Often, I find myself talking with people. And it doesn't have to be talking with people who are particularly qualified in the field of the work that I want to explore. I believe all people have something to contribute; sometimes, the unlikeliest people offer incredible insights and gems. Don't discount that.

Sometimes, I hear someone else's struggles and experiences relating to their feelings and ambitions. It may be that you can offer up some suggestions that help them catapult their progress exponentially, and they're forever grateful. Or maybe their struggle is your struggle clothed in a different way, and the support gained is symbiotic.

But I'm not just talking about making connections and networking where people are useful to you.

The next time you visit a local coffee shop, ask the person serving you if they're having a good day. Someone at the next table, give them a smile. Engage with the world, and the world will engage with you tenfold. We are not singular beings on this earth. We're a family. And families talk to each other. Just that little bit extra effort, just that little bit more listening, just that little bit more interest in other people will expand your world and give you a healthier mindset, more than you could ever imagine.

I know this for a fact from sitting for hours with my mum as a teenager, listening to her stories, listening to her worries; some might say, wow, that isn't what a teenager really should have been doing. But I couldn't do anything else but sit and listen. It was what I wanted to do. I wanted to help her. In some respect, I can see that now, in my patterns in life, I wanted to rescue her from this pain, but that wasn't my job. It took me years to understand that and quite a few therapy sessions to understand it wasn't my job to rescue her.

I realized that it impacted my relationships as I went through my early adult life. I would pick relationships where I wanted to rescue the other person, and it was my fault when I didn't manage to rescue them. I'd get the blame. I'd set myself up to fail. How curious is that? How curious is our behavior? I wanted to understand that more. And so, I ended up studying counseling; it took me outside of my comfort zone, and I grew. I learned so many things about myself.

So, have more conversations. Ask people how they are. Listen; when you need support and someone there to listen, everything will be there for you. The people will be there for you, and everything will fall into place. I guarantee it.

Chapter 21
How to Adopt the Habits of Success

You may have noticed that I've not mentioned very much about the types of struggles that you will come up against when you're persevering. People seem to like to focus on struggles and how to solve them. Yet, this isn't a book about how to solve problems. This is a book about cultivating the right mindset and the right habits for success in overcoming obstacles. Simply put, overcoming obstacles is done by having the right mindset and the right habits.

I think it's pointless to wait for problems and obstacles to come along and then deal with them when, in fact, you can be dealing with them as they arise at the moment.

The mindset that has been important to me is the mindset of never giving up.

Remember earlier when I talked about the origins of the book title because my son had picked up on the fact that I never give up on my dreams? I always keep moving forward. No matter what happens, I never lose my spirit of enthusiasm.

My enthusiastic attitude has become a signature trait that my coaching clients pick up on, too. They often comment on how contagious it feels and that it helps to drive them forward. You could say that my enthusiasm is leading by example.

My spirit of enthusiasm isn't just for one thing. It has been for many things in my lifetime. For my hobbies as a child, from starting my own business and building that business with only 50 pounds in my pocket at age 21. To grow that business, employ more than 100 people over a 12-year period. I Never Gave Up.

When my son said that to me, I smiled, and I thanked him and said, *"I had no alternative."* Because, in truth, what is the alternative? To never give up? Why would anyone want to give up? OK, don't get me wrong, this is not about blind ignorance, wanting to prove something to myself, or being stubborn, though at times I've probably been quite stubborn. It was always about excitement; that was the thing that got me out of bed in the morning; that was the thing that gave me the passion and the purpose to move forward. The excitement that manifested in enthusiasm was my secret weapon.

Whatever project you're working on, it's important that you feel that sense of purpose and passion, that enthusiasm. But where do you find it?

Every project starts somewhere. I remember when I started my first business, I would hand-paint t-shirts and take them along to the local university market on a Tuesday afternoon. There was someone selling secondhand clothes and another person selling ethnic jewelry. I remember every week, one very loyal student would buy one of my original T-shirts.

Each week, I felt excited because this loyal customer would buy one of my T-shirts; it was always the first sale of the day. Before I arrived, each Tuesday, I had already, mentally, made my first sale. This gave me a lot of confidence. And the great thing was, when other people saw someone standing at my stall buying things, it triggered the sheep mentality in other people. I would keep talking to him while he was holding his T-shirt. We'd chat about what he was interested in, and all the time, students would walk up and look at my T-shirts, and I'd sell another and another.

I would always get to a point in the conversation where I asked him, "What would you like on your T-shirt next week? And he'd give me an idea, he'd say what type of colors he'd like. He was so proud to have these T-shirts that were 100 percent original.

Sure, I'd spend quite a bit of time creating a T-shirt just for him each week, knowing that he was guaranteeing my first sale of the day. Spending a couple of hours on a T-shirt that had already cost me a few pounds wasn't very cost-effective, but I knew it was my first sale; I knew it would get my first customer, literally, through the door, and he would bring other people with him.

I didn't make a fortune on my t-shirt stall, but it taught me a valuable lesson, and that valuable lesson was never to give up. Always keep trying and exploring new and better ways of pushing your business forward. I knew I had a captive audience in this student, he taught me the value of over-delivering, by asking him what he would like on the next T-shirt. Every single week, I was guaranteed more sales than if I'd just stood there and waited for customers to come.

Okay, you're probably thinking 10 pounds per T-shirt. That's not a lot of money. But when you consider at the height, that business turned over a quarter of a million pounds per year. Hand painting t-shirts led to mass screen-printing t-shirts, printing fabric for fashion companies, printing posters and brochures, and designing corporate logos. Over a 12-year period, the business was built on my enthusiasm and mindset of never giving up.

Chapter 22
Beyond Your Master Plan

When we start something in motion, it continues in motion. Giving up means you're standing still. No business survives by standing still.

Okay, so I've talked about having a master plan and making sure that your master plan remains flexible. And how important it is to remain flexible. What I will talk about now is not your master plan but beyond your master plan because none of this has an end plan. There can't be an endpoint to your perseverance. To your passions, to your purpose.

The endpoint is ultimately the end of your life when you can do no more. and in some ways, it doesn't stop there because you may have created a legacy. That you've set something up those lives on after you've gone.

However, beyond the master plan, isn't about building a legacy. It's about gearing your interests, the time you spend doing and enjoying things that match up with and complement and resonate with your master plan.

I'll give an example. I'm passionate, as you know, about making cheese.

I wouldn't go as far as to say that I'm an artisan cheese maker - I'm not; I make cheese for myself and my family to eat at home and to share with friends and family. Taking that interest a step further, a few years ago, I planned a holiday to Italy. Everyone knows that Italy is known for its cheese-making, especially Parmesan. So, I decided we're going to Italy for a holiday, and we love food and trying different cuisines. Wouldn't it be great to visit a Parmesan factory to see how it's made?

I explored Italian food tours online and found one that was perfect. It described how we would arrive at the factory at 7 am to watch the cheesemakers start to make the king of cheese. For me, this was beyond exciting. Not only do I love making cheese, but the lifestyle that I've created and the holidays that we can enjoy also allow me to expand my interests and my dreams to expand my master plan. Think about it: not only do I make cheese and have the time and money to do that, but now I'm having a holiday, which is quite specialized, to tour a famous cheese factory.

Okay, so maybe that's not expanding the master plan that much, but let's consider this. Maybe one day I'd like to enter some of my cheese into a competition. There are cheese-making competitions all over the world. Wouldn't it be fabulous to enter a competition and take part and enjoy other people's passions and interests, taste cheeses, and be part of that whole experience?

Expanding it even further, how would I get there? How would I get to these different places that might be in Europe, based in the UK, how would I get there?

Another part of my master plan is to get my pilot's license. Can you see where I'm going with this? One day, when I've got my pilot's license and maybe my own small airplane, I can fly from my local airport to France or to Italy and visit cheese competitions or cheese markets. See how all of this ties in with my master plan. It feels like it's meant to be. Now, this may sound a little bit farfetched for some people.

Believe me, it's not. There's nothing farfetched about expanding your master plan and encompassing many other areas of your life and interests within it.

OK, back down to earth, another example from my life and my love of cheese involves a movie. I rarely watch mainstream TV, but I wanted to relax and watch something, so I thought I'd search for cheese-related films. I wasn't expecting to find anything, but I did a comedy.

It is a comedy and love story that involves cheesemaking. The film was very inspiring, it told the story of a cheesemaker who expressed a passion for making cheese how it impacted on his life and how he overcame many obstacles. It was a lovely, enjoyable story.

Instead of watching something random, I spent my time watching a movie about something I'm passionate about that fed into my interest, that fed into my enthusiasm. Can you see how all this links together?

Someone reading this might say, *"Maybe that's a bit obsessive."* Well, I hope so. I hope it's obsessive because that's exactly how I want it to be. Because for me, that's a healthy obsession. My mind isn't jumping from one thing to another. I don't feel like

I've got so many choices in life, I don't know which way to turn. I know exactly which way I'm turning. I know exactly how I want to spend my time. I know exactly where I put my energy, efforts, and money. Having that direction and that vision supercharges me and pushes me forward even faster because I can see a clear picture of the future.

While I'm out walking my dogs, I'll often see small, two-manned airplanes overhead from the nearby airport. I imagine that will be me one day. It may be that I've got a small airplane with some of my cheeses on board that I'm taking to a competition somewhere in the world.

That makes me smile because I know if I can think that it's possible, I can dream that it's a possibility, then I know it can happen, and I know I'm expanding my master plan.

Chapter 23
Be Grateful Every Day

How do you show your gratitude to the universe, the world, your world, and your experiences? Every day, when I wake up, I repeatedly repeat two words in my head. Those two words are THANK YOU. Thank you, thank you. I repeat those two words repeatedly while I lay in bed, slowly waking and entering the day.

Some years ago, I struggled with a business and lost everything. My business, my marriage, my home. I was financially broke. I was broke, and I was about to become homeless.

What I did have was a part-time job, and what I did have was time to study. Every morning when I woke and every evening when I went to bed, I had a small stone beside my bed. Maybe I got this small ritual from the book, The Secret, or the video.

And I would hold that stone in my hand and say to myself, *"This stone is a symbol of my gratitude. I accept that everything that happens in my life is because I chose it. And I realize it, and I accept it."* I did that every day for years. Throughout my life, I've always had small rituals that I've taken part in, just private and personal to me, from having a small pebble from the beach to just repeating two words. It doesn't matter what that ritual is.

What's important is that I take time out to acknowledge that I am grateful. I'm grateful for everything, not just the 'good' things. At the time, I had my more elaborate ritual, using my stone; I held onto that, literally held onto that, because I knew there was a greater plan in place. I knew that I was taking action to get myself out of that situation. I had a part-time job which gave me money to live, and I was studying; I was studying to do two things. Part of that study was to expand my knowledge, mind, and understanding of human psychology and the human condition. Studying counseling also helped me to study myself and understand myself.

Anyone who studied counseling will tell you that it's a two-way process. Not only do you learn the art and craft of counseling, but you'll also receive an awful lot of inner work. This was perfect for me at the time. Towards the course's end, I decided I didn't want to become a counselor. I was confident that I could do justice to the craft, but it was something that I chose not to do. I realized that studying counseling was more of a vehicle for me. It was a vehicle to get me where I wanted to be. It wasn't to be my destination.

I didn't know 100 percent where I wanted to be, but I knew that studying counseling was a vehicle to get me there; it resonated, and it felt right. What's important is that what we do is consistent with our thoughts. There's no point in doing something repeatedly, taking action when you don't believe in it. At the same time, there's no point in thinking one thing and doing the opposite. Because, at a deep level, you're sabotaging the outcome.

I believe our subconscious mind is very much like a child's. You confuse that child if you tell it one thing and do another. You're a poor parent. But if you do one thing and what you say and what you think is consistent, then the child/your subconscious gets a clear message.

The child gets a consistent message about what your intentions are and what you need them to do, and of course, every child pushes the boundaries to test, to test the parent.

If we do the opposite of what we say and think, we send out an inconsistent message that gets a confusing result. The last thing you need is a confused result because that's going to feed into all sorts of negative ways of behaving or thinking, it's dysfunctional, and it doesn't get you where you need to be.

When you consider what you're aiming to do and what your plan is, you need to ask yourself, *"Am I being consistent?"*

If someone is in a damaging, toxic type of relationship and yet they keep coming back to it and telling themselves the story that the good times outweigh the bad when they don't. They can't blame anyone else but themselves for continuing in that relationship.

I firmly believe that toxic relationships and problematic relationships are co-created because, if you take yourself away from the situation, no matter what the fallout is, if you take yourself away from that situation, things will change. It only takes one person to make that decision to say a very positive no, this must end. To remove themselves.

Chapter 24
Observe the Things You Do, Say, and Think

There are always consequences. There are always consequences to actions, there are always consequences to thinking differently. There are always consequences to things that you say. There's a school of thought, which I strongly believe is also. A school of thought says your words have power and magic in them. And that power and magic can be used for good or ill means.

So, observe what you do, look at what you say, and look at how you think. And ask yourself, are these things aligned with my master plan? Because if they're not, then it's holding you back. Now, you may think, well, I can't change how I think because I've always thought like this. And my advice would be, go and get some help. Go and get some support; go and talk to someone about it.

When people say, go and talk to someone about it, they often think, oh, that's going to be expensive, and I can't afford it. You can't afford to do it because things won't change until you become the change you want to see in your life. Also, there are services and organizations that will give you the help and support you need if you ask. It may be that they ask for a very small donation, one that's based on your income. Some organizations just leave an envelope on the desk, and they ask you to put what you can afford in that envelope.

So, align your thinking, your actions and your words with where you want to be. Think about the circumstances in which they might not be consistent. While you're doing something that's helping you move forward, helping you to persevere with something, it may be that you're telling yourself a different story. It may be that you're telling yourself this will never work.

What you're telling your subconscious when you say that is, this will never work, and you're right; it will never work if you hold on to those thoughts. It may be that you're saying those words to someone else. Someone is telling you you're doing really well. Everything seems to be working, going in the right direction; you should be really proud. And you come back with a self-deprecating statement like. *"Oh no, maybe not. Maybe it will end up the way it always ends up. And I'll almost get there, and then something happens and get in the way."*

The truth is, something already has happened. You've already said those words, and that's what's getting in the way. It's not external forces, the world conspiring against you, that get in the way. We get in the way of our own progress. The quicker you change your internal story, the quicker you'll get to where you need to be, where you want to be, and where you're destined to be.

The story we tell ourselves always has an outcome, and it's

important that we tell ourselves a consistent story with our words, actions, and thoughts.

A friend of mine will often say the same words to me: "Kev, you're living the dream." That always makes me smile. I'm living my dream. I'm living the dream to him, and maybe he can resonate with that, and his life is pretty good, too. But it makes me smile, and I'll say yes, I am living the dream. I'm living my dream. Because I know that my dream might be a nightmare for others. I don't have a flashy car, a big house, or a huge bank account. I'm not caught up with the millionaire mindset that tells me that success is measured by how much money I have or the social symbols that validate me to other people.

I personally take my sense of worth from an internal place. I use my own feelings to be my barometer to the way that I judge success. I ask myself, is there anything I'm suffering from now? Is there any pain in my life, and am I resisting anything now? And more often than not, my answer is no.

I've got lots of things that I'm working on, lots of things that I'm doing. I'd like to think that I've got things handled. The only reason that I can think that I've got things handled is because what I say, what I do, and what I think are aligned with my master plan. And as I've spoken before in this book, that master plan has ripple effects that spread widely and way into the future. I've also said the ripple effect can change direction because, just like a ripple on a pond, if that ripple meets up with something on the surface, it might be a leaf—it affects the direction of those ripples.

I understand that leaves do fall on the surface of life's pond. I accept that. I accept that, and because I accept that, I allow a degree of flexibility in my master plan. Because I understand that my master plan is part of the overall master plan. Of all human beings. And that interchange and dynamics… all come into play. And I'm okay with that, too. Because that means I'm engaged in life.

I know that the people I'm going to meet once I've written this book, and through web pages and my videos and audio, I know that the people I'm going to meet, some of them, will be there to support and help me. I know that some of them may want to take a part of me to help themselves.

And I'm aware of this. I'm interested and curious. I take the time to observe what's going on. I don't always get it right. Sometimes, my instinct is perfectly attuned. Other times, I say to myself, I didn't see that coming, but I learned from it. I learn from the experience. And all the time, I check to see if the words I speak, my actions, and my thoughts are consistent. That's the most important thing, and that, for me, is like having a survival pack while on the path, by being able to persevere and have the strength to carry on no matter what.

Chapter 25
Tune Out Those Destructive Distractions

There's no doubt that there are more distractions, more things to take your mind away from your priorities than ever before in human history. I remember all the way back to black and white TVs, to the test card during the afternoon when there were no programs on TV. When I look at society now, we have everything that we want streaming online 24/7.

You could say we're spoilt for choice. And spoilt is probably a good word that describes this. So, how do we countermeasure that side of our life? Because anything that gets in the way, anything that distracts us from our priorities or the things we really want to do, needs to be dealt with. Needs to be dealt with seriously. There's no pussyfooting around when it comes to distractions. Distractions must be met with equal or greater force to neutralize and remove them.

An example would be if you're a student who has many assignments or essays to get in on time, and you find yourself wasting hours on social media, keeping up with the news, and getting distracted by different posts and videos. One solution would be to turn off all your social media so it isn't pinging you every time you get a notification. To put your phone on silent. Now, that might seem like an easy, and certainly, often, that will do the job. But then you find yourself tempted just to have a look, give yourself a small break, and give yourself permission.

It may be that you need to take even more extreme measures. You may get to the point when you realize that the amount of time you can afford to spend online per day is possibly only one hour, and that's to do some research work.

The rest of the time, you need to knuckle down to do the writing, and this also occurs to anyone writing a book or article—of course, you need time to research, but the real meat of the work is when you get your head down and you physically do the work.

An extreme way of dealing with this would be to disconnect your internet, cancel your subscription to the internet, or physically turn off your internet on your phone.

Some readers might read this and think, shock, horror, where would I be without being connected? Well, think of it this way: where will you be if you don't get the work done? We can all justify, we can all tell ourselves that story that we might be missing out, but the greater goal is where you will be missing out.

If you only need a maximum of 1 hour online, get rid of your internet connection. I know that might sound extreme, but get rid of it. If you can't deal with having an internet connection at home where you do your work and you get constantly distracted and you're running out of time, then get rid of your internet connection altogether and cancel the subscription.

Then, find an internet café, a reliable internet café where you can go and do the work, to do the research. It's amazing how much work you do when you're blocking each job into compartments. You get so much more because you're focused on the job at hand. You become concentrated on your efforts, and you realize that you don't have a choice but to get the work done. Now if you find that you go to the internet café and instead of spending 1 hour there, you just trip over onto your social media and end up spending 2 or 3 hours there, another simple solution is to find out what time they close, find out what time they close, and if they close at 9 pm a night, don't go until 8 pm.

At 8 pm, you know you've only got 1 hour, and then the doors close, the internet is off, and you've got to get the work done then. Can you see how extreme this might sound? But these extreme measures are sometimes the only way to shift ourselves out of our bad habits. If you're tempted, take away the temptation. It makes sense because we can easily con ourselves. Humans are good at that. We have a devil on one shoulder and a devil on the other. And it's so easy to succumb, to say, we've done 2000 words today, why don't we have a little break, and then suddenly that slippery slope continues until you find yourself at the end of your deadline with only half of the work done and then you start to panic and wonder what happened.

Well, the reality is, you happened. You happened to let distractions get the better of you, and in a way, you can look at it like this. You are more committed to not doing the work and getting it done than you were to get it done. Again, you might think that sounds harsh. But the evidence is in front of you, you've only got 50 percent of the work done in the time that was available.

You've been more committed to not getting it done, and that's what happened. It was in your hands, you had control. So, if you didn't get the work done, you weren't committed to getting it done; otherwise, the work would've gotten done. It's simple. Now, people will be reading this section, thinking that I've gone off the rails here.

But I know this to be true. I have experienced it many times in my life, and it was only when I took extreme action that I overcame what I would call those weaknesses in my character. I overcame those weaknesses in my character, and at the end of it, I got the work done and felt much stronger for it. Not only did I feel much stronger about it, but it also built my confidence. Not only did it build my confidence, but it also made me realize that I have so much more potential. It expanded me.

Distractions shrink you. They shrink your potential; they shrink the amount of work that you'll get done, and they shrink your choices. That's what distractions do. And whether you call them distractions or obstacles, you know, you have more power to control these things than you give yourself credit for. In fact, if you don't give yourself credit for them, then you're just expressing the fact that you're more committed to not getting the work done because you're not giving yourself credit for the fact that you do have a lot of control.

Now, the procrastinators reading this will hear what I'm saying, and there will be a certain amount of self-loathing and a certain amount of resistance going on against what I'm saying, and that's fine. What's going on there is an interplay of negativity. But you need to step above this. You need to step above this, stand on your own two feet, and realize that your mobility depends on you taking the first step forward and taking positive action against these distractions.

Chapter 26
Parting Shots

Remember: DPS! No amount of good intention, visualization, or dreaming will outweigh the results of taking positive action.

"If there's one thing you've learned from this book – I hope it is, ***never give up****."*

Enjoy your incredible life!

Kev Webster

Printed in Great Britain
by Amazon